TO EVERYTHING THERE IS A SEASON

The Trials of an Appalachian Family

Book Three

BRENDA CRISSMAN MUSICK

Jan-Carol Publishing, Inc

TO EVERYTHING
THERE IS A SEASON
BRENDA CRISSMAN MUSICK

Published June 2016
Little Creek Books
Imprint of Jan-Carol Publishing, Inc.
Copyright © Brenda Crissman Musick

ISBN: 978-1-939289-99-5
Library of Congress Control Number: 2016945300

You may contact the publisher:
Jan-Carol Publishing, Inc.
PO Box 701
Johnson City, TN 37605
publisher@jancarolpublishing.com
jancarolpublishing.com

This book is dedicated to my seven grandchildren: Ethan, Haley, Landon, Logan, Leah, Nathan and Kiley. Each has brought "Nana" and "Gramps" laughter and joy in their own uniqueness. Ethan is beginning his career as a teacher, and I know he will do well, for he has a love and passion for his chosen walk. Haley has just begun the life of a wife as she also continues her education. She has a beauty that reaches to the depths of her soul. Landon and Logan are in college and still seeking God's direction. They will succeed for that very reason. Then there are the three still in elementary/middle school. I can't wait to see what God has in store for them...Leah, with the loving heart...Nathan, who loves the farm and sports and life...Kiley, who keeps us all entertained. May they find what God has in store for them.

And, as always, I dedicate this book to my husband. This past year has been a trial, and he has been there for me every step of the way. When I couldn't walk through the house on my own, he led me. When I was totally deaf for a while, he was my ears and mouth. When I felt I couldn't go on, he assured me I could and would. He has remained faithful to every vow he ever made. Thank you God, for this man you have given me.

ACKNOWLEDGEMENTS

I owe immense gratitude to my readers. You encourage me constantly as you talk about my books and the characters and ask, "When will the next one be out?"

I also owe gratitude to a dear friend of mine, Kathleen Taylor, who passed away last year. She was not only my friend, but my mentor and encourager. For the last two years when she was able, we traveled to our Reminiscent Writers Group together. We talked about growing up in the country, about our families and about writing. Her famous words to me and to others were, "Write it down!"

My greatest debt is to God. I cannot boast of anything I have done, for any ability I may have comes from Him. I believe when God gives us a gift, no matter what it is, we are to use it...and I have tried to do that. Without Him I would be nothing.

LETTER FROM THE AUTHOR

Dear Reader,

What a journey this has been! I set out to write a novel and somehow ended up with a trilogy. The Swank family had more to say than I realized. I hope they have become a part of your life as they have mine. I awakened one morning at 4 a.m., as I often do when writing a book, and God gave me the epilogue and last poem to this trilogy. As I lay in bed, the words of the poem taking root in my head, tears were streaming down my cheeks and I tried not to sob and awaken my husband. That's how important this family has become to me. Some might find that amusing, but I believe God wants us to have hearts of compassion. In fact, He commands us to "love one another" and with love comes compassion. Never be ashamed of your tears. My husband cries at sad stories and sad movies. For a while he tried to hide the tears from me, until I told him one day, "It takes a man with a heart to cry."

I know the Swank family has become a part of many of your lives. I'm constantly being asked, "When is the next book going to be ready?" (Music to an author's ears!) So many have said, "I just wanted to smack that ole One-Eyed Tom!" or "Carrie was such a good woman, but I wanted her to knock a knot on ole Tom's head." That bespeaks of folks who love to read and who get involved with the characters. Thank you for that.

Where do I go from here? Wherever God leads me! This past year I have faced serious health issues, at times wondering if the third book would ever be written. I have learned to take one day at a time and be thankful for the gift of each day. I have learned to appreciate God's healing and mercy. I have learned that God doesn't want a strong independent woman who can solve all of her problems on her own. God wants a woman who will rely on Him...and that's what I will do. Will there be another book? It's up to God.

In the meantime, keep reading! There are so many good authors out there...especially the Appalachian authors. You might even be one of them and not know it. Ask God to show you your gifts...and then USE them. It's been a joy!

Brenda Crissman Musick

FOREWORD

By Hazel Hale Bostic

Brenda Crissman Musick and I grew up with the same cultural background blessed to be surrounded by the love and support of our families. We've never taken for granted our Appalachian heritage, and remain true to traditional values. Brenda's writing reflects these country values of love for people and love for God

Her story of the Swank family demonstrates the typical life of most families of the Central Appalachia's in the early 1900s. They had their dreams and they had their troubles.

To Everything There is a Season reunites us with the Swanks. Who can forget *One-Eyed Tom?* We met him via Brenda's first novel of the same name. An unfaithful husband, Tom placed little value on his family. His misdoings bring consequences, but not just for him.

Brenda's second novel, *A Place to Belong*, continues the story of the sadness and pain inflicted by heartless Tom Swank upon his family. Through it all, Tom and Carrie's children search for peace and happiness. As readers we were left wanting more of the story, and Brenda certainly comes through for us in *To Everything There is a Season* as we reluctantly say goodbye to the characters who have become a part of us.

Hazel Hale Bostic is a widely published award-winning author, workshop presenter, and heads SWCC Reminiscent Writers.

To everything there is a season,
And a time to every purpose under the heaven:
A time to be born, and a time to die;
A time to plant, and a time to pluck up that which is planted;
A time to kill, and a time to heal;
A time to break down, and a time to build up;
A time to weep, and a time to laugh;
A time to mourn, and a time to dance;
A time to cast away stones, and a time to gather stones together;
A time to embrace, and a time to refrain from embracing;
A time to get, and a time to lose;
A time to keep silence, and a time to speak;
A time to love, and a time to hate;
A time of war, and a time of peace.

— Ecclesiastes 3:1–8 (KJV)

A MOUNTAIN WOMAN'S REWARD

The little house stands on the hillside,
Once shrouded in sadness and shame.
Its walls swollen from teardrops,
A man's selfish demons to blame.

His sins followed down through the ages;
Generations suffered his deeds;
But God in His infinite mercy
Looked down and saw all their needs.

He saw the faith of a woman,
The love of the children she'd born.
He said, "She deserves my best gifts
For the robe of beauty she's worn."

So he gave her the love of a good man
To stand by her through the years;
To hold her in times of trials
And kiss away her tears.

Now the house on the hill rings with laughter;
Its walls glow with warmth and rest.
The memories have found their rightful niche
With a love that stood the test.

— Brenda Crissman Musick

CHAPTER 1

S*omething's wrong with Nate. I can't quite put my finger on it, but something's wrong.* These were the thoughts rambling around in Carrie's head as she looked at her husband. Nate sat on the front porch in the rocker beside her, his head on his chest as he slept. *He seems to always be so tired, and he falls asleep the minute he sits down.* She watched him intently, the worry obvious in her eyes and her wrinkled forehead. Oh, how she loved this man...her husband for twelve years, now...the dearest man she had ever known. They had been the happiest years of Carrie's life. He was nothing like his brother Tom, her first husband and the father of her children. Nate was loving, giving, and unselfish—unlike Tom, who was filled with anger and always thought of himself before his family. Tom had brought his family nothing but heartache, his sins still invading their lives; Nate had brought it love beyond measure. Carrie's children adored Nate almost as much as she did, and he loved them as his own. *I don't know what I would do without him, Lord. He makes me laugh and he holds me when I cry; he is my rock.*

Carrie watched as Harold Moser worked in his little garden at the bottom of the hill, finishing the spring planting. He and Nancy were getting up in years, and their garden got smaller and smaller every year. Harold straightened and rubbed his back as Nancy came from the house, bringing him a drink of water. They were a happy couple despite the loss of two children in the past few years. Carrie couldn't even imagine the pain. They had been good neighbors through the years. She gave a little chuckle as Harold bent down and gave Nancy a kiss on the cheek. As though sensing someone watching, he looked up, saw Carrie, and waved, a big smile on his face.

Good folks, thought Carrie, giving a little sigh of contentment. They had always been there for her in times of need...and she had seen many of those times.

Her thoughts went back over the years of her life and the lives of her children. There had been sad times and tough times, but oh, there had been wonderful times, too. They were a family of love and joy. Even Luke and Jessie had finally found peace of mind and someone to share life with. She smiled as she thought about their marriages. Each one seemed like a miracle, since Jessie had vowed never to marry, and Luke had lost his first love...sweet, sweet Alice. Yet now they each had a devoted, loving wife and children whom they adored. *I'm like Grandpa Silas*, she mused. *I have more grandchildren than you can shake a stick at.* Carrie smiled just thinking about them.

She looked back over at Nate, his head still resting on his chest, and her mind went back to the day he proposed to her. He had been so nervous. *I love you, Carrie. I have for a long, long time...and I love you more every time I'm with you...and Carrie, I want to be with you all the time. I'll treasure you, Carrie, because you are a treasure.* Carrie almost laughed aloud just remembering. She had said "Yes" four or five times before he actually heard her. *Dear Nate*, she whispered inwardly. *God, please don't let anything happen to him.*

There was so much for which to be thankful; she didn't have time to dwell on the past. Thirteen grandchildren! She hugged herself with joy at the pure thought of those precious ones. Leah, her oldest granddaughter, was twenty-one now, and a teacher across the mountain in Baylor County. She would be getting married soon, to a young lawyer in the same county. Carrie had met him and had a good feeling about the match.

Nathan was the next oldest at eighteen, and such a fine young man. Ady Rose had three good children who had been raised in a home full of love. Nathan had been seeing a lot of Lissa, Homer and Trula's adopted daughter. Lissa had come to the orphanage when she was six years old, but wasn't adopted for years. At the age of twelve, Homer and Trula had adopted her into their family, which already had five children, and had given her the same love they gave the others. Lissa still worked at the orphanage. Ady Rose also worked there when they needed her since her youngest, Ethan, was twelve now.

Belinda had been told by doctors she would never have children, so she and Joe had adopted little Cammy, who was now thirteen. Then God intervened in all His mercy and gave Belinda and Joe another child. Carrie looked up at the clear blue sky as she thought of God and all he had done for her family.

Luke had gone through so much abuse from his father, and then lost his first love because of Tom. Carrie had feared he would never find happiness...but then Syrena came along...dear, patient, loving Syrena. Now they had two children and a home filled with happiness.

Jessie was the one for whom Carrie had most feared. He had so much hate in his heart for his father, and a deep fear that if he married, he might be like his father. Then Mandy came into his life, squelching all his fears and giving him three beautiful children. The hate was all gone and Jessie was a fine man.

Clay still lived on his horse ranch in Kentucky. He and Abigail had inherited the ranch after her father, Mr. McCleary, died. They seemed quite happy and content there with their three children and Carrie had made peace with her son living so far away, especially since she and Nate had begun visiting them a few times each year. All of Clay's children had taken to horses just like their parents, so she knew Clay would never return to the mountains to live. Happiness...that was all she had ever wanted for her children.

Then there was Cindy, her youngest, now thirty-three. How the years did fly! She and her husband Landon McLindy still taught in the school at Haymaker. Cindy had found out a few months ago that she was finally expecting, and just last week the doctor told her he was almost positive she would have twins. She and Landon were so excited. If the doctor was right, this would make Carrie and Nate fifteen grandchildren! Yes, her life was good.

Nate roused from his nap. "I must be getting old, Carrie. I fall asleep every time I get quiet. Will a beautiful young woman like you keep loving an old man like me?"

Carrie laughed. "I don't think either one of us can claim to be spring chickens, but Nate, I'll love you no matter how old we are."

Carrie had turned sixty a few months back, and Nate was now sixty-five. Age didn't matter much to her with all the joy in her life, but she had been concerned about Nate lately. He couldn't hold out to do half the work he did just a year before, and his shortness of breath concerned her. *I will not let myself worry*, she vowed to herself. *God will take care of us. I need to have stronger faith, and whatever He sends, He will give me the strength to handle.* She had been through many trials in her life, and she knew who to depend on for strength.

Nate reached over and took her hand. "It's still a miracle to me each time I wake up and see your face. I love you, my Carrie."

"And I love you, my Nate," she said softly. "You have brought me so much happiness."

It was mid-May, and one of the most beautiful springs Carrie could recall. Flowers were blooming, the trees were all in leaf, and their garden was planted. Even the air smelled good. Tomorrow would be Sunday, and all of the children and grandchildren would be coming for dinner.

All is right with the world, thought Carrie.

CHAPTER 2

The next morning, Carrie awakened to the promise of a glorious, sunny day. Nate was already up and had gone to feed the livestock. She hurriedly arose, washed, and dressed. Much of the food for Sunday dinner had been prepared the day before so that Carrie and Nate could go to the little church that Homer pastored, before everyone arrived for their usual family gathering.

I hope Lily will be there, thought Carrie, a sadness filling her heart. *I never thought I'd see my sister so sad and listless. She needs to get out of the house and be with people, especially family. Dent's been dead nigh on three years now, and she's still grieving. I wish I could help her, but I suppose everyone has their own way of dealing with pain.*

Dent had died suddenly of a heart attack while working at the orphanage one day, where he was custodian and handyman. There had been no warning. It had taken them all by surprise. Homer and Trula looked after her as much as they could, but with running the orphanage and pastoring the little Haymaker Baptist Church, their lives were busy. Besides, they had their own sorrows...

"Penny for your thoughts," said Nate, coming in the back door.

"Oh, just hoping Lily will be at church today. It would mean so much to Homer."

"Can't even imagine what they all must be going through," said Nate, shaking his head.

He set the milk bucket and eggs on the table and came to Carrie, his arms spread wide. She walked quickly into them and laid her head against his chest.

Nate kissed her cheek. "We just have to keep praying for their peace, Carrie love, and that the Good Lord will send Matthew back to them one day. Nothing is impossible with God, you know."

"Right you are," replied Carrie, giving him a hug and then walking toward the table. "Now I need to get busy, before time to leave. After church our clan will descend upon us with hungry, growling stomachs."

Hours later they returned from church and began putting the finishing touches on the meal. Lily had not been in church, and Trula looked as if she had aged twenty years. Carrie had invited them to lunch, but she and Homer had declined. Carrie was just stirring her dumplings when she heard the front door open.

"Where's my beautiful mother and that handsome man she wed?" called a female voice.

"Come on in, Ady Rose," laughed Carrie.

Ady Rose came into the kitchen along with Willie and Ethan, generously giving hugs.

"Leah, Nathan, and Lissa will be along shortly," said Ady Rose. "They wanted to drop in on Lily for a minute or two."

Leah had come home for the weekend, as she often did.

"Oh, wonderful," sighed Carrie. "Maybe she will come on to lunch with them."

Before anyone could say more, the front door opened again; Jessie and Luke and their families came in. Carrie stopped everything she was doing to give her children and grandchildren hugs. While hugs were still going around, Belinda, Joe, and their family arrived.

"Anyone seen Cindy and Landon?" asked Ady Rose. "They weren't at church today."

"Oh, I guess they'll be here," replied Luke, a sneaky look on his face. "Our feisty little Cindy is just moving much slower these days."

"I heard that!" called a voice from the living room.

Cindy came into the kitchen, walking slowly, with Landon right behind her.

Landon smiled and nodded to Luke. "Yep, a little bit slower."

Carrie gave her youngest daughter a big hug, noticing her growing stomach.

"How are you, dear?" she asked. "I was a little worried when you weren't in church. Everything all right?"

"Yes, Maw," Cindy replied, rubbing her back. "I just had a little backache and some nausea, so Landon wouldn't let me out the door. I had to do some fast talking to get to come here."

"Just taking care of you and my sons," said Landon, trying to appear the picture of saintliness.

"Sons?" queried Jessie. "Have you received a vision, Landon?"

Landon couldn't help but blush.

"No, just positive thinking. Actually, though, I won't mind one bit if we have girls. They will be good to wait on me in my old age."

The family was just getting ready to sit down to eat when Nathan, Lissa, and Leah arrived. Chairs were already out so they joined everyone at the table. After the blessing, the table was filled with talk and laughter as the food was passed around.

"How's the sheriff business in our fair town?" Luke asked, handing Jessie the platter stacked with fried chicken.

"Busy, busy," replied Jessie. "All the bank robbers are in jail."

"Uncle Jessie," said Ethan, a wrinkle in his brow, "has there ever been a bank robbery in Haymaker?"

"Not to my knowing," answered Jessie. "Haymaker is a quiet town, and I hope it stays that way. We did have a theft this past week, though."

"A theft?" gasped Belinda and Ady Rose in unison.

"Yep," said Jessie, shaking his head. "It got pretty tough there for a while."

"Tell us about it," urged Jessie's son Samuel, with the curiosity of a six-year-old.

"Well, it seems someone stole some of Miss Bessie's prize chickens. She was not a happy lady...and when Miss Bessie's unhappy, she don't want anyone to be happy."

Jessie spoke in a high-pitched voice, quoting Miss Bessie. "'You find them thieving hooligans and arrest them, Jessie Swank,'she said. 'That's what we pay you to do.'"

All ears were turned to Jessie now.

"Did you find the thief?" asked Lissa, forgetting all about the food on her plate.

"Well," answered Jessie, "it seemed hopeless there for a while."

"Then?" they all asked.

"Then one day, after two more chickens went missing, and after Miss Bessie had raked me over the coals again for not doing my job, I went looking again in the woods behind the chicken house. There I found feathers scattered everywhere, and a few bones on up the trail. I pretty well knew then it was no human that stole her chickens. I returned to Miss Bessie's back door."

"'Miss Bessie,' I said. 'I'm afraid the culprit here is not a person, but ole Red, the fox that shows up around here from time to time.'"

"Well, Miss Bessie just stood and stared at me."

"'So...,' she said, hands on hips and those lips drawn tight."

"'So...what?' I asked, not sure what else to say."

"'So get out there, Jessie Swank, and arrest that fox,'she said. 'I can't spare no more chickens!'"

At this, everyone at the table rolled with laughter. Nate looked over at Carrie and winked as if to say, *That's our family, Carrie love.*

After the meal they all retired to the front porch, except for some of the men, who decided to get up a game of baseball in the front yard. As the women sat enjoying the beautiful day, Ady Rose looked over at Carrie.

"Maw, I'm worried about Aunt Lily and Trula. They both just seem to get sadder and older everytime I see them."

"I know, Dear," replied Carrie. "I'm concerned, too. You know, not knowing about Matthew is, in some ways, worse than if they had just told her he was dead. Missing in action is a terrible thing. You wonder if they'll ever come home, and you also wonder what they are going through, if they are still alive."

"I remember the day the officers came to the door of the orphanage," said Lissa. "I knew the moment I saw them something was wrong, and Trula knew, too. Her face was ghastly white. Luke must have sensed something amiss as well, because he went running to fetch Homer. When they told them Matthew was missing in action, Trula didn't cry or anything. She just sat down in her rocking chair and started rocking. I've never seen her smile since that day. It was like the life just went out of her."

"If it was Nathan or Ethan, I know I'd be a basket case," said Ady Rose. "I wish there was some way I could helpTrula. Lily is no better. The life has gone out of her, too. I never thought I'd see her like she is now. She used to be so full of life."

"Just pray," said Carrie. "Just pray."

"I don't know if I'm supposed to tell this," said Lissa, "but Homer and Trula didn't tell us not to say anything..."

All heads turned her way.

Lissa continued. "Homer and Trula are going to give up their work at the orphanage."

"What?" they all gasped.

"Oh, what will we do?" cried Belinda. "We can't let Alice's Hope be closed."

"No," said Lissa quickly. "They don't want it to close. They asked Nathan and me to take it over. Trula said she can't deal with it anymore, and Lily's heart is just not in it."

"You and Nathan?" questioned Ady Rose, a little twinkle in her eye.

"Oh, I know I'm saying way too much, with Nathan not here beside me," said Lissa, wringing her hands and looking uncomfortable. "Maybe I should wait and let him say something."

"Could it be anything about a wedding?" asked Cindy, laughter in her eyes.

"Weelll..." stalled Lissa.

"Come on, girl. Out with it!" Cindy urged.

"We were going to tell everyone soon," said Lissa, blushing from head to toe.

This announcement was followed by hugs all around. Everyone loved Lissa, and this was really no surprise. She and Nathan were just meant for each other.

"So," continued Ady Rose, "do you think you and Nathan might take over the management of the orphanage?"

"We talked about it on the way here today, and I think we both like the idea. You know what the orphanage means to me. The only thing I'm worried about is that it will just give Trula more time to mope and worry. We'll need help: someone to cook, and a new handyman. Mark has been doing what he could, but he'll be going away soon."

"Going away?" Everyone else looked confused.

"Didn't you know?" asked Lissa. "He's going away to school; he wants to become a minister, like Homer. I'm really glad for him. He'll make a wonderful minister, and he needs to get away. There's so much sadness in their home. Even Martha tiptoes around like she's afraid any noise might upset someone, and she's only thirteen."

They all sat silently for a few moments, digesting all that had just been revealed.

Finally, Carrie looked at them all.

"Pray," she said, with a firm look and a nod of her head. "That's what we have to do, girls. Pray."

CHAPTER 3

The following Sunday, Homer had several announcements to make in his little church. Carrie was happy to see Lily there seated next to Trula.

"This is a blessed day for our family," began Homer. "Today I am happy to announce the engagement of our daughter Lissa to Nathan Crawford, son of Willy and Ady Rose Crawford, and grandson of Nate and Carrie Swank."

With this, the entire congregation applauded as Lissa blushed and Nathan smiled from ear to ear. Carrie glanced over to see Lily also smiling, but Trula just wiped a tear from her eye.

"The wedding is set for July thirtieth of this year," continued Homer. "However, there's more. As most of you know, Trula and I have talked for a long time about giving up our work at Alice's Hope. It is dear to us, but we aren't getting any younger, and it demands a great deal of time, time that I would like to give to my work here as your pastor."

At this people in the congregation looked at each other, nodded and smiled.

"As of tomorrow, Nathan and Lissa will begin working with us full time at Alice's Hope, learning everything about the daily running of the place.

Then, when they are married, Trula and I will retire and they will take over the orphanage. I have full confidence in their ability and dedication."

Applause filled the church once more.

"My mother, Lily, has agreed to stay on as cook for the orphanage, with the help of Lissa and our daughter Martha."

Lily smiled as the congregation applauded once more.

"We do need a custodian and handyman," added Homer. "Nathan has been filling that position in his spare time, along with our son Mark, but neither can continue in that capacity. And that brings me to my next announcement."

Everyone sat in silent anticipation.

"Our son Mark will be leaving in two weeks to go to divinity school in Hamrick County. He wants to follow in his ole dad's footsteps and become a minister."

This time the applause was thunderous, and everyone left the pews to shake hands and congratulate Mark.

"As you can see, our family has much to be thankful for. Times have not been easy for us in the past year, but God provides. No matter how much the pain, he is a just God, full of mercy and grace. Now let's praise him with song. Turn to page fifty-two, and let's sing 'Amazing Grace.'"

Carrie didn't know when she had heard "Amazing Grace" sung with such happiness and vigor. It was truly a joyous day. She just wished Trula could feel some of that joy.

As they left the church, she made it a special point to talk to Lily and invite her to dinner with them.

"Thank you, Sister," answered Lily, "but I have already promised to eat with Homer and Trula. Maybe you and I could eat at the diner one day this week. How would that be?"

Carrie could hardly believe her ears.

"That would be absolutely wonderful, Lily. How about Tuesday, around noon?"

They agreed on the time, and Carrie all but floated home. *Yes, it was one happy day!*

As Carrie set the table for dinner, Homer's announcements were all everyone could talk about. Nathan and Lissa, of course, received their share of teasing.

"Poor Nathan," moaned Jessie. "Most men get away from their wives every day, but he'll be working right along side her every single minute, of every single day, of every single week."

"It'll be constant nagging," chimed in Luke. "'Do this, Nathan. Do that, Nathan.' Poor man."

"That's enough, you two," warned Carrie, swatting them with her dish towel. "Now let's eat, and I don't want to hear anymore of that."

Her two sons took their places at the table, looking not one bit remorseful.

After the meal, the women remained in the kitchen to wash dishes and talk about the wedding. The men went outside to enjoy the sunshine—and to continue to kid Nathan.

"Lissa, what are your plans for the wedding, if you don't mind your future mother-in-law being nosey?" asked Ady Rose.

As Lissa turned around from the table, there were tears in her eyes.

"I don't really have any plans," she replied. "I know some things I want, but Trula just isn't in any frame of mind to talk about it, and I don't have anyone..."

With this, she broke into tears. The other women stopped what they were doing and sat down at the table with her.

"You most certainly *do* have someone," said Carrie, soothingly. "You have all of us, and we love you as if you were our own daughter."

Ady Rose sat down beside Lissa and took her in her arms.

"Lissa, I will help you in anything you want me to do. You are already my daughter, and I'm thankful Nathan has found such a wonderful woman to love. Now, let's just all sit here and plan this wedding."

"What kind of dress would you like?" asked Belinda. "We would be glad to make your dress in the dress shop...as a gift, of course."

Lissa gasped. "Oh, I couldn't ask you to do that."

"You didn't ask," replied Belinda. "I volunteered, and if I know Ady Rose, she is dying to be in on the sewing. So why don't we meet at the dress shop tomorrow? You tell us what you want, and we'll get started."

"Sounds like a terrific plan," agreed Ady Rose.

"I have an idea," injected Carrie. "We need to get Lily involved. I'm having lunch with her Tuesday. What if she and I make the wedding cake?"

13

"Oh, do you think she would do that?" asked Lissa. "It would be absolutely wonderful. I just want a cake. I don't know much about them, so why don't you and Lily just come up with something appropriate? I just can't believe this is all coming together. Thank you...all of you."

"Well," said Cindy, "I haven't come up with my part yet. What can a little round mother-to-be contribute to this special event?"

"Why don't you come up with a menu for refreshments and plan the decorations, with Lissa's input? Then assign each person something to make," said Ady Rose.

Cindy laughed. "I can do that! Teachers are good at planning and giving orders."

The rest of the afternoon was filled with the excitement only women can get from planning weddings. When it was time for everyone to go home, they all left with smiles on their faces and plans running topsy-turvy through their heads. The brightest smile, however, belonged to Lissa. She had found her place in this wonderful family.

"I believe my wife is a happy woman this evening," said Nate, standing on the porch, his arm around Carrie, as they watched the last of the children go down the hill.

Carrie laid her head on his shoulder. "Sometimes life is just good," she said.

She finished cleaning the kitchen while Nate went to feed all the livestock and milk the cows. Her mind was filled with the day's revelations, and anticipation of the days ahead.

Dear God, she whispered in her mind, *please use this somehow as a new beginning for Lily and Trula. Let them feel joy once more.*

On Tuesday, she met Lily for lunch at Lillian's Diner. Somehow, she could sense a change in her sister. It wasn't a big change, but something just seemed...lighter.

Thank you, God.

As they ordered and sat waiting for their lunch, Carrie began the conversation.

"I'm so excited about Nathan's and Lissa's wedding. They were just meant for each other. Don't you think so, Lily?"

Lily nodded. "Yes, I do. Willy and Ady Rose have raised a good son, and Lissa's one of the most loving young women I have ever known. You should see her around the children at the home."

Carrie reached over and took Lily's hand.

"I'm glad you are staying on at the orphanage to cook. Alice would be very proud of you."

"Oh, I don't know if she would be proud of me over the past few years," said Lily.

"What do you mean, Lily?" questioned Carrie, her brow wrinkling.

"I've not been much good to anybody since Dent died."

"Everyone has their own way of grieving, Sister," said Carrie.

"It just seemed like the life went out of me," declared Lily. "Then when Matthew went missing, I just got plumb mad at God."

Carrie squeezed her hand, waiting silently for her to continue.

"But in church Sunday, all of that changed," she said. "I promised God I wasn't going to mope any longer. There's too much to do, and I'm not too old to be useful."

"That is exactly right," agreed Carrie, "and I have something you can do soon."

Lily looked at her expectantly.

"You and I are going to make the wedding cake for Nathan and Lissa, at Lissa's request," announced Carrie. "How about it?"

Nodding her head emphatically, Lily replied, "Can't think of anything I would enjoy more."

Carrie began visiting Lily once a week, talking about the future and the wedding coming up. Lily liked to talk about Dent, and Carrie listened patiently, knowing it was good for her. Though she was doing better, there was still a marked change in Lily. She was quieter, more serious, and the raucous "Lily laugh" seemed to be gone forever.

It was after one of her visits with Lily that Carrie walked home one afternoon, her head a copious web of thoughts and plans. As she neared the yard gate she began looking for Nate, always anxious to see him after she had been away. He was usually sitting on the front porch waiting, but today his rocker was empty. Carrie walked through the front door and called out his name.

"Nate? Are you here?"

There was no answer.

He must still be out feeding the livestock, she thought as she headed for the back door, but there was an uneasiness in her heart.

As she walked out onto the back porch, her heart leaped to her throat. Nate was slumped over on the porch steps.

"Nate? Nate, Darling, are you okay?"

When she touched him she saw he was drenched in sweat, his skin cool and pallid.

"I caaann staa uh," he answered, his words slurred and unrecognizable.

Kneeling down, Carrie put her arms around him and just rocked him back and forth. She had never felt so scared.

"Nate, let's see if we can get you in the house, my darling."

With her pulling and tugging, and Nate giving what little assistance he could, she was able to get him into the house and to their bed. She lifted his legs onto the bed, removed his shoes, and pulled the covers up to his chin. He was shaking uncontrollably, so she bent close and put her arms around him.

After a few minutes she said, "I'm going to get some water and a cloth, Nate. I'll be right back."

Dear heavenly Father, she whispered as she made her way shakily to the kitchen, her heart thumping loudly, *please don't let my Nate die. Help him, please—and God, if you would, send someone to help me.*

Carrie quickly returned to the bedroom with a pan of water and a cloth. She applied the cool cloth to his head, whispering words of comfort and love.

"I doon knnn whaaa..."

Nate tried to talk, but the words just wouldn't form. He shook his head from side to side in frustration. Carrie feared that he had had a stroke.

"Colll," he said, and Carrie realized he was trying to tell her he was cold. She hurried to get more quilts to put over him.

Just then, someone called out.

"Maw, are you home?"

It was Jessie.

Oh thank you, God.

Carrie ran to the bedroom door.

16

"Oh, Jessie. I have never been so glad to see someone in all my life. Something has happened to Nate."

Jessie followed his mother into the bedroom. As he looked at Nate, anxiety registered on his face. Carrie could see the fear in his eyes.

"What is it, Maw? What's happened?"

Turning from Nate, Carrie whispered, "I fear it's a stroke, Jessie. We need to get Doc White over here as soon as possible. Can you go get him?"

Jessie gave her a quick hug. "I'll be back with him in no time. Now don't worry, Maw."

He leaned over and squeezed Nate's shoulder.

"I'm going to go get the doctor, Papa Nate," he said reassuringly. "Don't you worry about a thing."

He quickly hurried away and Carrie sat down on the bed beside the man who had brought her so much happiness. She could not stand to think of losing him. She began to pray.

"Father, I know you give and you take away, and I know you have a perfect plan, but right now I'm asking for your mercy. I haven't had Nate long enough. Please let me keep him a while longer. I need him, God; more than you do right now, I think. My family needs him, too. He is a dear, sweet man, and a true gift to me, Lord; he makes our family complete. So if you can send me some mercy right now, I'll forever be beholden to you. Thank you, God. Amen."

As she ended her prayer, she felt Nate's hand wrap around hers, and as she looked up, his eyes looked straight into hers and tears slid down his rugged old cheeks. He squeezed her hand, and Carrie smiled and kissed his tears. She felt a sudden peace.

"It's going to be all right, my darling Nate," she said, and Nate nodded his head.

"Did you hear what Jessie called you? He called you Papa Nate. That's how they feel about you, Darling. You are the father they never had, and they all love you."

Jessie soon returned with Doc White. After a thorough examination, the doctor confirmed her fears.

"I'm afraid he's had a stroke," he said. "But Carrie, I don't think it's a severe one. The only think that seems to be affected is his speech. His reflexes are good, and nothing seems to be paralyzed. "

"Praise God!" exclaimed Carrie, the tears falling unchecked. "Do you think he'll be okay, Doc?"

"Well, only time will tell," Doc White answered, "but I have no reason to think otherwise. The next forty-eight hours will be crucial. Usually when it's only the speech that's been affected, they recover completely—even the speech. It will take time, however, and patience and work."

"Oh, I can be very patient," said Carrie.

"It's not your patience I'm concerned about," said the doctor, nodding toward Nate. "I'm afraid it's Nate's patience that will be tested."

Carrie rubbed Nate's hand.

"I will see that he is patient, and we'll both work to get him back to normal. God is giving us more time. That's what matters."

The doctor nodded. "Right now, and for the next several weeks, he needs rest, and lots of it. Do you understand me, Nate?"

Nate nodded his head.

"For two weeks I want bed rest and chair rest. Nothing beyond that. Is that understood? Do not lift anything heavier than a fork."

Again Nate nodded.

"If you are doing well after two weeks, you can take short walks—with assistance. In the meantime, you can be working on your speech, and reading the Good Book won't hurt none. I feel that your speech will come back if you work hard and exercise patience. Now I'll be back day after tomorrow, unless you need me sooner. I'm giving Carrie some medicine to keep you and your heart calm."

CHAPTER 4

Carrie was true to her word during the next weeks. She worked diligently with Nate as he tried to utter words, failed, and tried again. Sometimes he became upset with himself; other times they both laughed at his efforts. One night as they lay in bed, Carrie was helping him with his speech.

As they rested a moment, Nate looked over at her with a twinkle in his eye. "I gwa I mawy Cawry."

Carrie began to giggle and soon Nate was laughing, too. "I'm glad you married Carrie, too," she said.

After the two weeks of rest ordered by Doc White, they also worked to build his strength back. Each day one of the children came and helped with his therapy. The boys took him on daily walks, making sure he learned to use his cane, while the girls worked with his speech and laughed and talked with him. Carrie often stood at a distance and smiled. These children certainly loved Nate. In agreement with all concerned, Willy took over the daily running of the farm except for milking Ole Bessie and gathering eggs, jobs Carrie adopted. Life was filled with getting Nate back to health and preparing for the wedding. All in all, it was a happy time; Carrie had an inner peace, trusting in God to take care of Nate.

It was a Monday and Belinda had come to work with Nate. Carrie left them on the front porch and went inside to attend to her washing and baking. Nate's appetite was returning, and she joyfully made his favorite foods. As she kneaded her bread dough, she thought she heard singing and wiped her hands to go check it out. There on the porch sat Belinda and Nate, looking out over the neighborhood and singing.

"Row, row, row, your boat, gently down the stream..."

Carrie could hear Nate; his voice strong, but the words came out, "Woe, woe, woe ooor boat..."

She smiled to herself as she watched Nate. She could see a smile on his face as he proudly belted out the little tune, and Belinda was smiling as if she had accomplished the greatest of feats.

Thank you, God, for your mercy and your love. You are using this for good, Lord, and I do thank you.

Carrie went back to her baking, humming as she worked, "Row, row, row your boat..."

Later that day, as she and Nate sat on the porch side by side in their rockers, he reached over to take her hand. As she looked at him, he said, "Wuv oo, my Cawy."

"And I love you, my Nate," she replied, not even trying to stop the tears.

On a beautiful, sunny Saturday in July, Nathan and Lissa were married. Homer beamed from ear to ear as he performed his adopted daughter's ceremony. Mark, the oldest now that Matthew was away, gave the bride away. He had obtained special permission to return home from seminary to attend the wedding. Luke and John stood up with Nathan as Martha and Leah stood with Lissa. Carrie sat proudly by Nate, thankful for the progress he was making and that he could be there with her today. After the wedding, a reception was held at the orphanage, Alice's Hope. Carrie couldn't help but think of how Alice would have enjoyed this day. She had been very special in their lives, and had made the most of her own short life, although it had been one filled with pain and loss. Carrie's reminiscing was halted as Nathan stepped to the front of the room.

"Lissa and I want to thank all of you for sharing this day with us. Most of you have shared our entire lives. I want to thank my parents for all they have taught me, and for their unfailing love. We want to thank Homer and Trula and their family for giving Lissa a home, a family, and their love. We will be gone for a week, and then we will return to take over the running of Alice's Hope. Lissa and I are going on a very special mission this week, with Homer's and Trula's blessing. Most of you don't know this, but for some time Lissa has been trying to trace her birth parents. The search has led us to Kentucky, and we are going there to see what more we can learn. From there we will go on to visit Uncle Clay and his family. We ask your prayers that God will help us find what He wants us to find, and that He will bring us safely back to the place and people we love."

After hugs, handshakes, and much back thumping, Nathan and Lissa took their leave. Carrie and Nate stayed to help clean up and then Luke drove them home. It had been a wonderful day and Nate had made it better than Carrie could even have hoped, although she could sense his fatigue as the day drew to an end. The cake she and Lily had made had turned out beautifully, and Lily had seemed happier than Carrie had seen her in a long time. Even Trula smiled lightly a time or two.

The following week took on its routine, as life has a way of doing. On Monday, Willy came to work on the farm and stopped by the house for a glass of cold buttermilk. Later, Luke came to walk with Nate, whose strength continued to grow; he was even stronger than before the stroke. He didn't really need the boys to walk with him anymore, but it seemed to be something the boys needed to do for their own joy, so the walks continued. On Tuesday, Ady Rose came to work with Nate on his speech, and they both insisted that Carrie get out of the house awhile and go visit Lily, so she took her leave, knowing that Nate was in good hands.

Lily was working at the orphanage each day while Nathan and Lissa were away, so Carrie made her way there to visit with her sister for a while. As she entered through the back door, she heard unexpected laughter.

Is that Lily? She asked herself.

Carrie walked into the kitchen to see Lily talking with a white-haired man who was leaned on the sink, his eyes twinkling as he laughed with her. Lily blushed as she looked up to see Carrie.

She looks just like she used to when Mama Cynth caught her reading romance novels, thought Carrie, quite amused.

"Good morning, Lily," she said. "Ady Rose is working with Nate this morning, so I thought I'd come visit my sister. Is this a bad time?"

Lily blushed again, and Carrie could hardly hide a mischievous smile.

"N-not at all," stammered Lily. "Carrie, this is Floyd Roberts. He has hired on as our new custodian and handyman. Floyd, this is my sister Carrie."

Floyd smiled and doffed his hat like a gentleman, and Carrie couldn't help but take to him. Besides, if he could make Lily laugh again, that was reference enough for her. He quickly took his leave.

"I'd best get back to work, so's I don't get fired on my second day of work," he said. "You sisters have a good visit now. Good to meet you, Carrie."

With this, he doffed his hat once more and left. Lily turned quickly back to her work.

"Hmmm..." said Carrie.

"Hmmm, what?" said Lily. "Now Carrie don't you start on me. He's new here, and I was just trying to make him feel welcome. That's it, and that's all."

"Hmmm," repeated Carrie, smiling wickedly. "I think he was feeling welcome, all right."

Lily looked at Carrie, hesitated, and then both sisters broke into laughter.

"He does seem like a nice man," said Carrie. "I'm definitely glad they found someone to help out around here. What do you know about him?"

Lily, continuing with the cake she was preparing for the oven, looked serious.

"I don't know a lot. He's from Rockville, just over the line in Kentucky, and he's sixty-eight years old. He just lost his wife a year back, and they had no children, so he's pretty much alone. I think he's hoping to start a new life here."

"Well, then, we'll just help him do that," said Carrie emphatically.

She spent about an hour with Lily, picked up a couple of items at the mercantile, and then headed home. It was good to get out, but she didn't like to leave Nate for long. As she walked up the hill she could see Ady Rose and Nate on the porch, and as she drew closer she could see a little table spread with a cloth, and food set out.

"Come join us," called Ady Rose. "We decided to have a picnic."

Sure enough, there were sandwiches, lemonade, and cookies, laid out in picnic fashion. One look at Nate and she could tell he was in seventh heaven, as he smiled from ear to ear. She bent to kiss his cheek.

"Sit down, Maw," commanded Ady Rose. "There's plenty for three."

They ate and talked, and Carrie told them about Floyd Roberts.

"Wouldn't it be super if Lily got herself a beau!" gasped Ady Rose.

"Now, let's don't get ahead of ourselves," admonished Carrie. Than with a twinkle, she added, "But it could happen."

After they finished eating, Carrie noticed out of the corner of her eye that Ady Rose gave a questioning look to Nate and then Nate very slightly nodded his head.

"Maw," said Ady Rose, "Nate has something he would like to say to you."

Carrie looked at Nate expectantly. He took her hand and looked into her eyes.

"I l-l-love y-you, my C-Ca-rie," he said.

She could hardly believe her ears. He had said it as plain as day!

"Oh, Nate," she gasped, not even bothering to wipe away the tears. "Oh, Nate, my darling Nate, I love you, too."

Carrie could not remember a happier moment, unless it was the day he had proposed to her. God had given her the best man on earth. After another hug for Nate, she threw her arms around Ady Rose, whose face was wet with tears of joy.

"Thank you, my sweet daughter. You have given me the greatest of gifts."

CHAPTER 5

Nathan and Lissa returned happily from their honeymoon, ready to take over the management of Alice's Hope. They had a custodian and handyman now that Floyd had hired on, and Lily was helping with the cooking, but they needed more help and were trying to find a woman to help with the cooking and the general housework. Lissa had not found the answers she was looking for as to her birth parents, but she had found some leads and she was not giving up. As she was doing laundry at the orphanage one Monday morning, there was a knock at the kitchen door. A woman in her late twenties or early thirties stood on the porch.

"Hello," Lissa greeted her with her usual gentle smile. "Is there something I can help you with?"

The woman stood there a moment longer, as if wondering what to say. Then she gave Lissa a nervous smile.

"I hear you are looking for some help here," she said.

"Why, yes, we are," said Lissa. "Come on in, and I'll pour us a cup of coffee. That is, if you like coffee."

In her heart, Lissa was breathing a sigh of relief. It was not unusual for an unwed mother to arrive on the doorstep of the orphanage looking for a place for her unborn child. Sometimes it was a woman whose husband had left her and she had no way to support herself or her child. Lissa didn't mind having new children come in, but it broke her heart to see children separated from their birth parents. After all, she had been one of those children. However, that did not seem to be the case with this young woman.

The woman walked through the door that Lissa held open.

"Yes, I like coffee just fine."

As they walked into the kitchen, Lissa noticed how tired and thin she looked.

"I was just about to sit down to a blueberry muffin," she said. "Won't you have one with me?"

The lady simply nodded her head, but Lissa saw relief in her eyes.

"Now, my name is Lissa. My husband Nathan and I run the orphanage, along with some help. And your name is?"

As she talked, she set the coffee and two muffins in front of her visitor.

"My name is Mary...Mary Carlisle," she said before taking a bite of her muffin. "I'm from over in Kentucky. I was raised in an orphanage myself."

"Oh, is that so?" gasped Lissa, eyes widening. "So was I. In fact, I was raised in *this* orphanage, until the owners adopted me at the age of twelve. Were you adopted?"

"No," Mary replied.

Lissa waited for her to add to her answer, but she said no more.

"Are you married?" inquired Lissa. "Do you have a family?"

Mary looked uncomfortable. "No. I have no one. My husband died two years ago, and I've been making it on my own. My last job was in a boarding house over in Kentucky. It didn't pay enough to live on, but they did give me a room and food."

Lissa nodded. "Please understand. I'm not trying to pry, but I have to know a little about the people we hire. For instance, I need to know if you have other responsibilities such as a home of your own and a husband or children to take care of outside of this job."

"I have no one," answered Mary, quietly. "I can give this job my full attention."

Without further questions, Lissa continued. "The job here would include helping with the cooking, cleaning, and washing—a never-ending job. Also, you would be needed to help with the children at mealtime."

She went on to tell Mary about the pay and about the town.

25

"We have a boarding house here in town, run by one of the dearest ladies you could ever meet. Her name is Sarah McLindy. Her rates are very reasonable and meals are included, or you are welcome to have your meals here. On your days off, I think you could find some part-time work, if you still needed the money. Do you sew?"

Mary's eyes seem to light up for the first time.

"Yes, I'm quite accomplished with the needle and thread, if I do say so myself."

"The lady who owns the hotel and dress shop is my husband's aunt," said Lissa. "I can take you to meet her, if you decide to stay and take on the job here."

They talked for a while longer, and Mary agreed to take the job.

Lissa phoned Sarah McLindy at the boarding house and arranged a room for Mary. Mrs. McLindy agreed to wait for the first week's rent; when Mary received her first pay from the orphanage, she would pay Mrs. McLindy.

"Let me go hang these clothes on the line, and I will show you around our facilities," Lissa offered.

Mary reached down and picked up the basket of clothes.

"Why don't I hang these up while you tidy up the kitchen?"

Without waiting for an answer, she headed for the door.

In the weeks to come, Mary proved to be a wonderful asset to the orphanage. She was kind and loving with the children, seeming to come alive in their presence. She and Lily got along well, although she would have nothing to do with Floyd. He tried in every way he knew to be friendly, but Mary seemed to take an instant dislike to him. In fact, she was reserved around all men.

"Mark my word," said Lily to Lissa one day, "that woman has been hurt by a man in her life."

True to her word, Lissa took Mary to meet Belinda. When they went into the dress shop Mary's eyes grew round, as if she had just discovered a pot of gold.

"I can see you appreciate the beauty of creating things with your hands," observed Belinda. "I know the feeling. Have you used the needle all your life? Can you also use a sewing machine?"

26

Mary nodded eagerly. "My mother taught me to sew at an early age, and yes, I can use the sewing machine."

Lissa looked perplexed. "I thought you grew up in an orphanage."

A flush crept from Mary's face to her neck. "I did grow up in an orphanage, but not until my mother died. I was eight when she passed on, and there was no one to take care of me."

Belinda sat down on the settee and took Mary's hand. "I am so sorry, Mary. I can't imagine how hard that must have been. I've had my share of trials in life, but I always had a loving mother."

"Yes, you are quite blessed," replied Mary.

Belinda saw something in her eyes she could not explain. What was it? Pain? Anger? A longing? *She has suffered something awful in her life*, she thought.

When they left the hotel, Belinda had given Mary a job on Wednesdays, her day off, plus any work she could handle at nights and in her spare time. Ady Rose was helping Belinda that day, and filled Mary in on the story of Alice's Hope and its importance in all their lives. Both Belinda and Ady Rose seemed to like Mary, who was a little reserved, but friendly. In fact, they both invited Mary to come to church Sunday, and then to go with them to Maw Carrie's afterwards. Mary accepted both invitations.

The November Sunday morning dawned sunny and bright with just a hint that fall had dropped in for its scenic stay. Leaves made fluffy mounds on the ground everywhere, but enough remained on the trees to brighten the little community with gold, orange, and red. It was hard to believe that Thanksgiving would be here in just a few weeks. Lissa and Nathan arrived at church with all the children from Alice's Hope, which now boasted a total of fifteen children. Mary came with them, a little girl holding each hand as they took their seats just in front of Carrie and Nate. Lissa had wanted to introduce them before church, but they were seldom early with fifteen children to get ready. Introductions would just have to wait, as Brother Homer was stepping to the podium.

"Good morning, my friends," he said. "Isn't it a beautiful day to be in the house of the Lord?"

Several "amens" rang out.

Carrie glanced over at Trula, who sat stone-faced with her children and Lily. She also noticed that Floyd sat just behind them.

"Let's begin our worship today by praising God in song. Turn to page four hundred, 'Love Lifted Me'."

With this, everyone broke into song. At the end of the first verse, Lissa realized she was hearing a beautiful soprano voice; it was Mary! As she sang her face took on a glow that warmed Lissa's heart. She glanced at Carrie, behind them, to see if she had noticed. Carrie smiled and gave a slight nod.

As soon as she gets a little more used to everyone, we'll have to ask her to do a solo, thought Lissa. *I believe our Mary is going to be an important part of Haymaker.*

After the service, and after shaking hands with friends and the pastor, Nathan and Lissa waited with Mary outside the church. Lily, Floyd, and Martha, Homer and Trula's daughter, were taking care of the children and the orphanage that afternoon so they could have the Sunday meal with Carrie and Nate. As Carrie came outside, Lissa waved to her.

"Maw Carrie," she began, "I want you and Papa Nate to meet our new friend and worker at the orphanage. This is Mary Carlisle, from Kentucky. Mary, these are Nathan's grandparents, Carrie and Nate Swank."

Carrie couldn't help but smile at Lissa's introduction, and Nate was beaming from ear to ear. She reached out to take Mary's hand.

"Welcome, Mary," she said warmly. "I'm so glad Nathan and Lissa have found some help, and from what I saw in church, the children have really taken to you."

"Maw Carrie," said Nathan, "we also invited Mary to eat with us at your house today. We told her how much you love people at your table."

"And right you are," laughed Nate, nodding his head. "Mary, you will make this lady very happy if you come have lunch with us."

Mary nodded and whispered, "Thank you."

Carrie couldn't help but notice that her demeanor changed when Nate spoke. There was almost dislike in her eyes.

Goodness, she thought, *I've never known anyone to dislike Nate. People usually take to him like a child to candy.*

They all headed toward the little hillside home, and Mary's reaction to Nate was soon forgotten. Mary mostly listened as all the children and grandchildren talked and laughed, but on occasion Carrie saw her talking with Belinda or Ady Rose. She also saw her looking around from time to time, with a searching or longing in her eyes. Carrie couldn't quite put her finger on it, but she knew something had happened in Mary's life to cause a deep-seated sadness.

If anyone can take away that sadness, thought Carrie, smiling, *it will be these children God has blessed me with. Thank you, Lord.*

As they sat around the large dining table, talk and laughter abounded.

"Cindy, is the doctor still sure it's twins?" asked Lissa. "It's not much longer now, is it?"

Cindy squirmed uncomfortably in her chair. "No, not much longer, and this gal is ready. I waddle like a duck, and haven't had a good night's sleep in weeks. And yes, he is still saying twins. I'm pretty sure he's right, from all the commotion in here."

She rubbed her stomach as she talked.

"Do you think you'll miss teaching, little Sis?" asked Luke.

"I doubt that she'll have time to miss it," answered Landon before she could speak. "I may have to quit teaching myself, with two to take care of."

"Very funny," laughed Jessie. "You'll be anxious to get out of there every morning, with all the noise."

"While we're on the subject..." said Landon, glancing toward Carrie. "We were wondering, Maw Carrie, if you would come help Cindy for a while after the boys are born?"

"*Boys,* is it?" inquired Carrie, a twinkle in her eyes.

"He keeps insisting he knows it is boys," said Cindy, shaking her head. "I guess he's become a prophet."

"Just wait and see..." Landon said, stroking his chin.

Carrie smiled at their banter. "To answer your question, I will definitely come and take care of my grandsons. In fact, if it's okay, I plan to come and stay a couple of weeks. Nate will come help also, during the daytime after he finishes his chores. How is that?"

"Oh, Maw!" said Cindy, with a deep sigh. "That will help so much. I have to admit, I'm a little nervous about being a mother—and more than a little nervous about twins. Thank you, and thank you, Papa Nate."

"Don't forget your big sister," said Ady Rose. "I can help, too."

Then the talk turned to farming, news from the town, and Thanksgiving. Carrie smiled as she looked around the table. Her family was finally happy.

After lunch, the men and children headed outside to enjoy the nice weather, tell their tales, and talk about farming. The women gathered in the kitchen to do dishes and talk about the things women like to talk about.

"Syrena, I hear Mary Alice is excelling in her school work," said Cindy. "I wonder if we may have another teacher coming on in our family."

Mary Alice was the oldest child of Luke and Syrena. At age ten, she loved school and could never get enough of reading and learning—unlike her younger brother, Jacob Troy, who at age seven, would much rather be climbing a tree or throwing a fish hook into the creek.

"We are proud of her," replied Syrena, "but I don't know about teaching. She insists she will be Haymaker's first woman doctor."

"Wow!" the women all said at once.

"I believe she can be anything she sets her mind to," vowed Carrie. "That reminds me...Cammy told me the other day she wants to help run the dress shop when she finishes school, and maybe even open a millinery. Has she talked with you about it, Belinda?"

Belinda glowed as she answered. "Just last week, she came to Joe and me with her thoughts about it. We are *thrilled*. Joe is already planning where we might add on a millinery. Cammy thinks it should be an extension of the dress shop."

"I think a millinery would do well in Haymaker," said Ady Rose. "All the women seem to be wearing hats these days, especially to church."

As they talked, Carrie noticed Mary's quietness. She seemed to be taking in every word, but said very little.

I guess she just needs time to get to know everyone, and feel a part of our town and our family, she thought.

Suddenly, as if knowing Carrie's thoughts, Mary spoke.

"I love this table, Miss Carrie. It is beautifully made, and just fits your family, and the children seem to enjoy eating at their own table in the adjoining room. I especially love this bench on the backside of the table."

"This table is very special," answered Carrie. "It was made by Nate's father, Paw Charles. He made it for me and my first husband when we set up housekeeping."

Mary had turned a ghastly pale.

"You were married before Nate?" she asked. "Oh, I'm sorry. I didn't mean to be nosy."

Carrie patted her hand. "You are not being nosy. Yes, my first husband died."

Mary made no reply, but sat rubbing her hand over the table, a puzzled look still invading her face.

Carrie studied Mary for a moment. *I might as well be honest, if I want her to feel a part of this family,* she told herself.

"My first husband was not a good man, Mary," said Carrie. "He caused pain for me and my children...but it didn't stop there. Sin never hurts just the one doing the sinning. It hurts many people. But then God gave me a good man. I hope you will learn to like Nate, Mary. He is the best of men."

Mary didn't reply for a few minutes, but just as Carrie started to rise and go back to her work, she asked, "So you married your first husband's brother?"

The girls all looked questioningly at each other.

"Yes," replied Carrie. "After many years, and I've never once regretted it."

"Papa Nate has brought so much love to this family," said Ady Rose. "He's the father we always should have had."

"I guess we had better be heading back to the orphanage," injected Lissa, seeming to feel the conversation should end there. "I know Lily and Martha will want to be getting home, and Floyd could use a little rest. He works so hard for us each day. He's really been a blessing."

Mary rose and moved toward the living room.

"Thank you, Miss Carrie, for inviting me to lunch."

"You have a standing invitation," said Carrie, placing her arm around Mary's shoulders. "I hope you will come any Sunday you can."

"I will see you on Wednesday," said Belinda to Mary. "I want to introduce you to Nettie Willis. She wasn't there when you came the other day. She works in the hotel, and also sews for us in the shop. She's been with us several years."

"I'll look forward to it," answered Mary. "Thank you, everyone, for making me feel at home."

As they stepped out onto the front porch, the men stopped their conversation.

"Looks like we're headed home," said Nathan, reaching to take Lissa's hand.

Nate stood from his rocking chair. "I'm glad all of you came. Come back every chance you get...and Mary, we are especially glad you could join us today."

Mary ducked her head and did not reply, but Carrie noticed she did not turn pale this time. *Better a little progress than no progress,* she thought with a smile.

CHAPTER 6

The Sunday before Thanksgiving dawned with an undeniable chill. Fall chose to deceive the little Haymaker community no longer. As Nate finished his milking and feeding, Carrie, ready for church, put the finishing touches on their Sunday meal. As far as she knew, all the children would be there, unless Cindy wasn't feeling up to it. Even Lily had agreed to come.

Carrie smiled, a little mischievous smile. *She doesn't know I invited Floyd to eat with us.*

Ady Rose and Willy came by to pick them up as they usually did, except on warm days, when they enjoyed the walk. As they arrived at the little Missionary Baptist Church, quite a crowd was gathering; everyone had a hug or howdy for them. Homer had just arrived with Trula, Luke, John, and Martha. He always had a smile on his face, though Carrie knew there was pain inside. Trula was unable to hide her pain, and while Carrie understood, she could see Trula had allowed her pain to affect the lives of her children, who always seemed so sad. Nate made it a special point to talk to the boys.

"Well, now, Luke," he said, putting his arm around the boy's shoulders. "What's this I hear about you liking to work with horses?"

Luke just gave a nervous smile and nod.

"He really does, Papa Nate," injected Martha, when she saw Luke's reluctance to talk. "He's really good with them, too."

By this time everyone was moving on into the church and Carrie gave his arm a tug, so Nate said no more. He did intend to pursue the matter, though; an idea had been taking root in his head...

They moved to their usual pew and took their seats as Homer stepped up to the pulpit.

"I was glad when they said unto me..." quoted Homer.

And the congregation continued, "Let us go into the house of the Lord."

"There is no better place to be, my brothers and sisters," said Homer. "God's house is a place of love...a place of worship...a place of healing."

Carrie couldn't help but notice that Homer looked out of the corner of his eye at Trula. *They all need healing, Lord,* her thoughts whispered.

"Let's stand and worship the Lord together with hymn number sixty-seven, 'Come Ye Thankful People.'"

After the hymn, the small children went up front to sing a song as proud parents beamed. Then there was quiet as they returned to their seats. Everyone prepared themselves to listen to the sermon, but Homer remained in his seat. Instead, Sarah McLindy remained in her place at the piano, and Floyd rose and proceeded to the front. As Sarah played, Floyd stepped to the pulpit and began to sing "Great is Thy Faithfulness."The congregation could not believe the sound of his beautiful baritone voice. Nate looked over at Carrie and smiled.

When the song ended, everyone broke into applause. Floyd, red-faced, took his seat and Homer stepped to the pulpit.

"O give thanks unto the Lord; for he is good: for his mercy endureth forever," quoted Homer from the Bible. "My friends, *that* is to whom we need to give thanks. We need to thank him every day for his blessings and especially for his mercy. We have so much to be thankful..."

At this point Homer stopped. The congregation sat waiting, but he did not continue. His face was drained of all color. Carrie heard the door to the church squeak a little as it was opened or closed. She wasn't sure which. Homer's eyes were frozen on the doorway, and the entire congregation turned to follow his gaze. There stood a young man: maybe twenty, or a little more—it was difficult to tell. His face was bearded and worn, and crutches held him upright. Someone in the church gasped, and from her side vision, Carrie knew it was Trula. Then she saw Luke and John grab their mother, who had stood up, to keep her from falling. About this time Carrie realized who the young man was.

"Matthew?"

It was Homer's voice; he left the pulpit and made his way down the aisle. Tears poured rapidly down his cheeks. Trula still stood in the front, held up by her children, as in a trance.

"Matthew, my son, my son!" shouted Homer. "You've come back to us!"

He threw his arms around his son, and they both sobbed.

"Oh, Papa," cried Matthew. "It is so good to hear your voice."

They held each other again and cried. Then Matthew walked to his mother.

"Mama, it's me...Matthew," he said quietly, as if speaking to a child. "Don't you recognize me? I'm home."

With this, Trula seemed to rouse from her state of shock. She smiled for the first time since they had received word that he was missing, and it was like she couldn't stop.

"Oh, my darling boy," she said softly, rubbing her hand on his cheek. "I feared I would never see you again."

She put her arms around him, and he embraced her. They stood there, just quietly holding each other tightly, as if to make sure each was real. His siblings stood to the side in wonder, tears flowing and highlighting the smiles. Then the entire church was on their feet, greeting Matthew and sharing in the joy as only a church family can do. After a few minutes, Ike Millard stepped to the pulpit.

"Brothers and sisters, I think we need to let Pastor Homer and his family go home now. They have a lot of catching-up to do. Brother Homer, take your family home. We'll finish out the service here. We have some praising the Lord to do!"

Without further ado, Homer and Trula turned with their family to leave. Suddenly, as if remembering something, Trula turned and went back toward the front. She took Lily by the hand, leading her out with them. She then stopped at the pew where Lissa and Nathan stood.

"Lissa, you are our daughter, too."She took her hand, and Nathan followed.

Homer walked over to Carrie and Nate.

"This is family time," he said, "and you are family. Will you come with us? We all need to rejoice as a family and hear Matthew's story."

"We would love to come with you," answered Nate, taking Carrie by the arm.

The little home where Homer's family lived was just a short walk down the dirt road from the church. As they walked, no words were spoken, as if they were all just trying to take in this glorious event. Matthew walked with crutches; his mother's hand was on his back the entire time, seemingly afraid that if she didn't touch him, he might disappear.

"Would you like to have lunch before we talk?" Trula asked as they entered the house. "I have plenty for everyone."

Matthew seated himself on the sofa, placing the crutches on the floor to the side.

"I'm not very hungry, Mother," he said. "Could we just talk a little first? We have quite a bit to catch up on."

Without another word, everyone took a seat.

"Son, are you sure you are up to this?" asked Homer. "As long as we have you, the story can wait. We don't want to tire you."

Matthew shook his head. "No, Papa. I've been looking forward to this day...forever, it seems. There were times I almost gave up hope, but I remembered all you taught me about trusting in the Lord, and somehow I just kept going and believing."

He swallowed, cleared his throat and continued. "I was in the battle at Normandy. Have you heard of that battle?"

No one seemed able to answer, so Luke spoke. "Yes, Brother. We've heard of it. After they told us you were missing, we read everything we could about the war, just hoping something would jump out at us or lead us to you. Yes, that battle was an awful one."

"Well," continued Matthew, "I was in the battle at Omaha Beach. I can't remember too much about it, except I was scared to death. I remember, Papa, when you used to read to us from the Bible about David, when he hid in a cave. I would think David was a coward and wasn't trusting in the Lord, but believe me, that day I changed my mind. I wanted to serve my country and I wanted to fight for justice and freedom, but that day I wanted nothing more than a dark cave to hide in. But there was no cave, so I fought alongside my comrades."

He stopped for breath, the battle coming alive once more in his mind. Martha handed him a glass of water and he took a sip, then continued.

"I remember the awful noise...planes overhead, bullets ringing in my ears. I remember seeing soldiers fall and others stumble over their bodies, pushing onto the beach. Then I remember something jarring my whole body, and the jarring was followed by terrible pain. I remember suddenly seeing Mama's face."

Trula gave a soft whimper and Matthew took her hand.

"After that, I recall nothing of the battle. In fact, a long period of time is missing from my memory. The next thing I remember, I was waking up in a little house and I could smell the wonderful aroma of broth or soup, and I felt so hungry."

"Where were you?" gasped John, impatient for the rest of the story.

"Shhh," cautioned his father, patting his shoulder.

"I was in a home in Belgium, in a little town called Tournai. I have no idea how I got there, except for what I was told. Tournai is just over the border from France. The house I was in was owned by an elderly man and woman named Ilson...a wonderful couple. There were Germans in the area, so they had to hide me in a small, concealed back room. They said I was brought there by some British soldiers, who drove up and just left me at their door. I had been shot three times, and had lots of shrapnel in my body. They doctored me themselves. They were amazed that I lived, but Papa, they believed in God, and even before I fully regained consciousness I had this feeling that someone was praying for me. At times I even heard their voices. I know it was God who saved me, through the love and kindness of those dear people."

"We owe them a great debt," said Homer, wiping tears from his cheeks

"I don't know how long it took the British soldiers to get me there," said Matthew, "but I had been with the Ilsons two weeks before I finally awoke. I have been with them ever since, waiting for money and a way to come home."

"Didn't you notify the Army?" questioned Luke

"I did just recently," answered Matthew. "It was the Army that finally brought me home. It was over a year before I healed from my wounds enough to get around, and there were other circumstances..."

Everyone looked at him, waiting for him to go on.

Matthew took another drink of water, hesitating to continue. Then he looked at Luke.

"Luke, would you go over to Mrs. McLindy's boarding house and tell her I said 'okay?'"

Though perplexed, Luke nodded and left.

Matthew continued. "The Ilsons took such good care of me, feeding me when they had little food for themselves. It was a difficult time in Belgium, then. Though many of the Germans had left, there were still small groups who would show up from time to time. They would ask how many lived there, look around a bit, then take all the food they could find. Eventually, however, I didn't hide anymore and could go outside for exercise. I could even help some on their little farm."

As he spoke, Luke came back into the house and nodded to Matthew, a glow on his face.

Matthew smiled at him. "What I haven't told you is that the Ilsons had a daughter. Her name is Anja, and Mama, Papa, she is your daughter-in-law."

Everyone gave a gasp as Luke walked back to the door and opened it. A beautiful young woman walked shyly into the room and stopped by Matthew's side. He reached up and took her hand.

"This is my Anja," he said to everyone there. Then he simply waited.

There was absolute silence for a moment as everyone tried to process the news. Then Trula rose from her chair, walked over to Anja and took her in her arms.

"Welcome, my daughter," she said. "We are glad to have you in our family."

This greeting was followed by a warm hug from Homer, and then one by one, they all welcomed this lovely, blue-eyed young lady into their family.

Eyes sparkling, Martha said, "Well, tell us the rest of the story, Matthew. You can't stop here. How did you fall in love? Does Anja speak English? When did you get married? Are you home to stay?"

As she finally ran out of breath, everyone broke into laughter.

Laughing, Matthew looked at Anja, and it was easy to see the love in his eyes. As the family looked at Anja, they could see that love reflected in her eyes.

"Yes, we are home to stay," answered Matthew. "Yes, Anja speaks English, for I have been teaching her. We fell in love while I was living in their home. When the German soldiers would come to the house, she had to hide with me in the concealed room so they wouldn't harm her. To keep her mind off the danger, I taught her English. She was a fast learner. She helped nurse me back to health and we walked together every day, building back my strength. We were married six months ago. Now I just need to find a job, and we need a place to live. Right now Sarah McLindy is spoiling us at the boarding house, but we can't live there forever."

"I'm sure we can find you a job in time," said Homer. "You need to rest and get better, first. As far a place to stay, your mother and I have an extra room that has been waiting for our son to return. Will you come live with us, until you are able to work and have a place of your own?"

Matthew looked questioningly at Anja. She smiled and nodded.

"Thank you," he said. "We would love to live with you for a while, as long as you let us do our share of the work."

Carrie, Nate, and Lily had said little. It was a time for Matthew's family, and they were just happy to have heard his story. After a few words with Homer, Trula, Matthew, and Anja, they took their leave. Carrie and Nate walked Lily home.

"It is amazing how God works things out," said Carrie. "We often give up too soon, not realizing His greatness."

"Right you are, Sis," agreed Lily. "Right you are."

CHAPTER 7

"Nate! Wake up!"

Carrie was shaking Nate, trying to rouse him from his sleep.

"What is it, Love?" he asked groggily.

"I smell smoke," Carrie answered. "Something's on fire!"

Nate hastily jumped up and dressed. Carrie already had her robe on. They hurried first to the kitchen to see if something was on fire, but nothing was burning there. Just then, movement outside the kitchen window caught their eye.

"The barn!" cried Nate. "The barn's on fire!"

They hurried out the back door and toward the barn. Carrie stopped, picked up a bucket and headed toward the pump.

"We'll need water!" she shouted.

Nate turned and looked back, then shook his head.

"No, Carrie, my love," he said, taking her arm. "It's too far gone. Water won't help."

They stood sadly and watched it burn, feeling a loss almost like that of an old friend.

"Thank goodness there were no animals inside," Nate finally said.

"But the hay is all lost," sighed Carrie.

"We'll have more hay," answered Nate. "Let's just praise God that no lives were lost and it wasn't the house."

"But what could have caused it? You haven't even been near the barn since this morning."

The fire was too hot to get closer to the barn, so they stood in silence, holding each other. Later, after Nate had milked and Carrie fixed breakfast, they sat at the table eating in silence, at a loss for words.

"Maw? Papa Nate?"

It was Ady Rose's voice, and she looked worried as she, Willy, and Ethan came hurriedly into the kitchen."Maw, what happened?" she asked. "We were on our way to town and smelled the smoke. I couldn't believe it when we realized it was coming from here, and I was afraid it was the house. Thank God you are both all right."

Ethan came and put his arm around his grandmother.

"We don't know what happened," answered Carrie, holding Ethan close. "I smelled smoke and woke Nate. We saw through the kitchen window that the barn was on fire, but it was too late to do anything. No one had been in the barn since yesterday morning. Nate milked last night, but that was near the tool shed. We just don't know how it started."

"What did you lose?" asked Willy, in a more practical realm.

Nate motioned for them to sit down as Carrie brought the coffee pot and some cups.

"Well, we lost quite a bit of hay...and the plow was in there. I think that's about all. The bridles and such, and most of the tools, are in the tool shed. There may have been a pitchfork or two."

Willy nodded. "That's not too bad. We'll have to order a new plow before spring. It won't take too long to rebuild the barn, with plenty of help."

"I volunteer," said Jessie, coming into the kitchen. He walked over to his mother and gave her a hug. "Word travels fast, and Mort Ramey told me about the fire. How about if we drink a cup of coffee and then I'll go with Papa Nate and Willy to look at things? I think Luke's on his way."

Sure enough, Luke showed up moments later; the men, along with Ethan, went to look over the remains of the barn.

"Please be careful," admonished Carrie, as they headed toward the barn.

"Maw," said Ady Rose, "if you don't feel like having Thanksgiving dinner here Thursday, we can have it at our house. Everyone will understand."

Carrie shook her head. "No, dear. We've celebrated Thanksgiving in this old house for many years, even when times were not good. Just because the barn's gone doesn't mean we'll stop. Family is much more important than an old barn. Besides, we have so much to be thankful for this year. I'm sure Homer and Trula will celebrate Thanksgiving at their own home with their family, and Lily will join them, but we can still thank God for what He has done for them. And just look how He has restored Nate's health. No, a barn burning will not get in the way of our joy."

The men said little about the barn when they returned, reeking of smoke, and Carrie assumed they would probably never know what caused it.

"We won't do any building this Saturday, since it's Thanksgiving weekend," said Jessie, "but we can go ahead and be cleaning up out there. Then the following Saturday, weather permitting, we can gather all who can help and have a barn raising. I can be here bright and early this Saturday for cleanup. Who can join me?"

Luke, Willy, and Ethan all agreed to be there.

Thanksgiving was a happy, peaceful time for Nate, Carrie, and their family. The following Saturday, all the men in the family and a large number from the little neighborhood and town showed up to build a barn. Homer and his boys came, and although he couldn't do any carpentry work, Matthew came along. The men soon had him sorting nails and even sawing small pieces from time to time, and he took to the work with vigor as his face displayed a smile of satisfaction. Around noon, women began to show up with food to feed the hungry carpenters.

"This is just like how people used to help each other," remarked Belinda. "We are blessed to have such good friends and neighbors."

A faraway look came into Anja's eyes. "We use to do this, too," she said in broken English. We had a good village, before the Germans came."

Syrena put her arms around Anja. "I'll bet you're feeling a little homesick right now, aren't you?"

Anja ducked her head. "A little, I suppose," she whispered.

42

"Have you thought about bringing your parents over here?" asked Ady Rose.

"Yes," said Amanda. "They would like it here, and I know they would be welcome."

"We have talked about it," said Anja, "but we have no money right now, and it would all have to be worked out. It would be hard for Mama and Papa to leave their home, and they are not young anymore. Still, I would so like to have them with me, especially…"

She said no more, but Carrie saw a certain emotion in her eye, and thought she knew what Anja was thinking. When in a young woman's life did she most want her mother with her?

The barn was finished just in time. The following week it began to snow, and it continued on and off for several days. The little town of Haymaker and all the neighborhood snuggled in, waiting for the snow to cease so they could get around without the slipping and sliding of winter time. Those who had to go out to work found a way to do so. Others used the time for cooking, cleaning, quilting, and whatever needed to be done. There was always work to be done in the mountains and hills of the Appalachians. Christmas soon came, and then was gone, and life continued on.

It was toward the end of January, with about eight inches of snow on the ground. The sun had beamed bright and early, and Carrie was hoping for some melting of the glistening white blanket. At mid-morning there was a knock at the door.

Well, who on earth made it out in this weather? she thought.

The door opened just as she got to it, and Jessie peeped inside as he stomped the snow from his boots.

"Jessie, what are you doing out in this snow?"

Stepping inside he gave her a hug. "Well, Maw, I came to get you. It seems our Cindy has picked this cold, icy day to go into labor. If you'll get your things, I'll take you to her. Where is Nate?"

"He's shoveling snow away from the back porch and trying to make a path to the barn. Let me go tell him what's going on."

"Why don't I go tell him, while you get some things together?" suggested Jessie. "It will take us a while to get back to town. I'm sure there's plenty of time, but I'm also sure Cindy is wanting her maw right now. The doc is with her and so is Mrs. McLindy, but she wants you."

"I'll hurry," said Carrie, heading toward the bedroom as she spoke. It made her think back to the cold snowy day when Ady Rose was born. She had been all alone with two little ones, but God had sent Ben to help. Dear, sweet Ben: Nora's Ben, how she missed him.

Soon she was ready to leave, after making Nate promise not to overdo the shoveling and to come into town the next morning after his chores were done, if weather permitted.

"Now, Jessie, you be careful with your maw," warned Nate. "I don't want anything a'happening to her."

Jessie and Carrie left with assurances to Nate that they would take the utmost care. It was all Carrie could do to walk in the snow, holding on to Jessie for dear life. When they reached his truck at the bottom of the hill, she was glad to climb inside. But the going was not easy; a drive that usually took ten minutes ended up taking nearly thirty. Finally they arrived, happy to see that someone had cleared the path leading to the house. Carrie removed her galoshes and coat and headed to the bedroom to find Cindy propped up on pillows, Sarah McLindy sponging her forehead.

"Oh, Maw, thank goodness you're here," cried Cindy.

"It looks like you are getting the best of care," replied Carrie, giving Sarah a hug and bending to kiss her daughter's cheek.

"Yes," said Cindy. "Mother McLindy is taking such good care of me, but I just needed my mama here with me."

Mrs. McLindy patted her shoulder. "A girl always needs her mother at a time like this."

"Where is Doc White?" inquired Carrie.

"He has been here," answered Sarah, "but he left to check on another patient. It seems another baby has picked this day to join the world. Doc will be back in just a bit, and he assured us there is plenty of time."

At this moment a pain hit, and Cindy moaned loudly.

"Maw, I just don't know if I can do this!"

Carrie laughed and took her hand. "Well, daughter of mine, I don't think we can cancel things now."

Cindy smiled weakly. "I know I'm being weak and silly, but I'm just so scared."

Squeezing her hand sympathetically, Carrie said, "All women giving birth feel the way you're feeling, my dear, but when you hold those babies you'll forget all about the pain and fear. Now just lie back and relax. I'm right here with you, and I'm not going anywhere."

Over the next few hours, the pains came more and more frequently. Doc White returned, checked her progress, smiled, and nodded.

"Looks like those babies will get here before dark today, and everything is going as it should. You just rest as much as you can between pains, and if Sarah will get me a cup of coffee, I'll see if I can't be ready for the big event. You wouldn't want ole Doc to fall asleep right in the middle of things, would you?"

With this he gave a roaring laugh, amused at his own words. "Now you and those babies just hold off, and let an old doctor have his coffee."

"Can we come in?" called a voice from the living room.

Without waiting for an answer, Belinda and Syrena walked into the room as Doc White left. "How is my baby sister doing?" asked Belinda, bending down to kiss Cindy. "Mandy sends her love and will be over in a bit."

"I have been better," answered Cindy, to which her sister laughed.

Syrena smiled. "We can certainly relate to that feeling, but I promise it is worth every pain. How much longer does Doc say it will be?"

"At least until he has his coffee," groaned Cindy, with a cross look.

The others laughed.

"He says before dark," replied Carrie. "I wish Mama Cynth was here, like she was for so many in this town. I remember how I hated it when she had to go away, but I was so proud of her."

"Tell us about her, Maw," urged Belinda, both because she wanted to hear about her grandmother and to take Cindy's mind from her pain.

Carrie smiled just to think of her mother. "She was about the dearest Christian woman you could ever know, and Papa Silas loved her with all his heart. With her dying words she told him she loved him. There was always a sadness in his eyes after she died. She would go out to birth a baby no matter the weather, or even when she wasn't well. Often it would be the tenth or eleventh baby she had birthed to the same couple. Sometimes she got paid with a hen or a slab of ham, or maybe some flour or meal, or whatever the family could afford, but she didn't care about that. Many families had nothing to pay her. Mama often stayed two or three days with the mother and baby, if there were complications. She—"

About this time a hard pain hit, and Cindy cried out. This brought Doc White back into the room, no cup of coffee in sight.

"If you ladies will step into the living room, I will check our progress," he said. "Of course, Miss Carrie, you can stay."

He checked Cindy with positive sounding "uh-huhs" and "okays" as he did so.

"I believe these little ones are in a hurry to get here before dark," he announced. "Is everything ready for them? Blankets, bassinettes...all that stuff? I've had my coffee and I'm good to go."

Carrie smiled and nodded. "Everything's ready, Doc."

"Then you go get Sarah, reassure that nervous father-to-be, and tell the others it's that time. Tell 'em to have some coffee. They should hear some squalling pretty soon."

Thirty minutes later, little Daniel Landon, named for his father, was born, making his entrance into the world with a red face, a head of dark hair, and a loud cry. About five minutes later, David Charles joined him, with equally strong lungs. Each was quickly cleaned, bundled and handed to his tired but beaming mother.

"Oh, Maw," she said, as tears trickled down her cheeks. "Oh, Mother McLindy, look at your new grandsons. Landon was right all along; both are boys. He's going to be so proud."

"Well," said Doc, "don't you think we'd better invite the proud father in to see his sons?"

Sarah went to get Landon, wiping a tear from her eye as she thought about how much the Reverend would have enjoyed this moment. The proud papa literally glowed as he held one and then the other. Finally he looked at Cindy, with a scared expression on his face.

"Cindy, how will we ever tell them apart? I can't see a single difference."

Not only had she given birth to twin sons, she had given birth to identical twins.

"Just tie a name tag on each one's big toe, boy," said Doc White, then walked out laughing.

Landon gave Carrie and Cindy a confused look. They both broke out in laughter.

Sarah McLindy patted her son's shoulder. "He was only joking, Son. Don't worry. You'll soon find differences."

Carrie stayed on with Cindy, Landon and the twins for almost two weeks. Sarah came to help when she could, but she had a boarding house to run. The other girls dropped by to stay for an hour or so each day, but they too, had their own homes or jobs. Carrie didn't mind. In fact, she loved holding and changing her new grandsons, trying to find ways to distinguish between Daniel and David. Cindy was up now, feeding and helping care for the boys. Nate came and stayed most of each day, and then went home before dark. That was the hardest part. It was the first time Carrie and Nate had been separated. On Carrie's last day, she approached Cindy with an idea.

"Cindy, I know you are getting stronger every day and can do a good bit of the work, but with two babies I think you need some help. What would you think about hiring Anja to come a few hours each day for a while? I know they could use the money, and it would make her feel more like a part of the family."

She didn't add what she was thinking. *I think she's going to need the experience.*

"Yes!" squealed Cindy. "I've been trying to think of someone. Maw, could you go ask her before you go home? Tell her if she's interested to come right over and we'll talk about it."

Carrie went immediately to Homer's house. Anja was very receptive to the idea, and agreed to go right over. Before the day was gone, Anja had a job and Cindy had some help. Carrie rode home with Jessie feeling content, and anxious to see her Nate.

CHAPTER 8

February gave way to March, and March pranced in with sunshine and warmth. Carrie was back home with Nate and ready to begin the things of spring. Spring was always a time when she felt a special joy in her heart, excited to see the newness of life all over again. Nate had bought a new plow and had already begun preparing a garden. The jonquils and hyacinths were giving a sneak preview of their beauty. Soon Carrie and Nate would be sitting on the front porch once more.

Carrie remembered how they use to sit on the front porch on Saturday evenings when Nate came a'courting. She remembered the first time he reached over and took her hand. He didn't say a word, just held her hand. What wonderful memories she had, and she was anxious to make more.

The twins, almost two months old, were doing well. They were growing by leaps and bounds. It was still hard to tell them apart. Matthew and Anja had finally announced that they were going to be parents—not a surprise to Carrie. Homer and Trula could not stop smiling. They had their son back, a new daughter-in-law, and now there would be a grandchild. From what Carrie could hear, Floyd was visiting Lily quite often and Lily had learned to laugh again. Lissa was still trying to find her birth parents, but as of yet had found nothing. Mary Carlisle had proven herself a wonderful asset at the orphanage, and in the little dress shop. She and Nettie Willis worked well together and had become good friends.

After talking an idea over with Carrie, Nate had written a letter to Clay. He had received a quick response and planned to take the next step. They had arranged to talk with Homer and Trula after church on Sunday.

Carrie was taking some clothes from the line, fighting to hold on to them in the March wind, when Nate came from the barn. He hurried over to help her.

"We may have to go to Haymaker to pick up some of those if you let them go," he laughed, taking them from her arms.

He started toward the house; Carrie picked up the basket and clothespins and followed. "What would I do without you?" she said.

"You couldn't," he answered. "I'm worth my weight in gold."

With that, he reached over and planted a kiss on her cheek.

They had just reached the door when they both came to an abrupt stop.

"What's that?" asked Carrie, though she knew.

"Sounds like the fire siren in Haymaker."

Immediately visions of their burning barn stole into Carrie's head. "Oh, I pray it's nothing serious."

A few hours later, as they were having lunch, a knock at the door was followed by Willy's voice.

"Maw Carrie? Nate? You here?"

"Come on in, Willy," Carrie called. "We're in the dining room."

"Would you like to have a sandwich with us?" asked Nate, as Willy came in. "We're eating light today, but Carrie makes the best egg salad in the land."

"Thanks, but I'll have to be getting on home," said Willy. "I just stopped by with a bit of bad news."

"Oh, no!" gasped Carrie. "Is it about the fire, Willy? We heard the siren earlier."

Willy took a seat. "I'm afraid it is. It was Lily's house."

Both Carrie and Nate gasped.

"How bad was it?" Nate asked, reaching for Carrie's hand.

"Thankfully not as bad as it could have been. Bert Wilkins happened by just in time to see the smoke, and got the firemen out quickly. The kitchen is pretty bad, but the rest of the house is okay. Like I said, it could have been a lot worse."

"Thank God for that," whispered Carrie. "What about Lily? She'll need a place to stay."

"She's going to stay at the boarding house," answered Willy. "Homer and Trula don't have any room, with Matthew and Anja living with them. There was a room at the orphanage, but Lily turned it down. She didn't say, but I think she felt it was inappropriate with Floyd staying there. I told her me and Ady Rose would be glad to have her stay with us, but she wanted to stay in town so she could keep working at the orphanage. All in all, I think it will work out. Mary Carlisle is staying there, and we all know Sarah McLindy can make anybody feel good. Besides, I think the house can be repaired in two or three weeks."

"Do they know what caused the fire?" asked Nate.

Willy shook his head. "Not yet. They know it started in the kitchen, but they have to look things over more. Well, I'd best be going. Just wanted to let you know about it."

Carrie rose with Willy. "Thank you so much for stopping by. I'll try to get to town tomorrow to see Lily."

She stood watching Willy walk down the hill to his truck, a worried look on her face.

Nate walked up and put his arm around her, lovingly running his finger along the wrinkle in her forehead. "I know something's going on in that pretty head of yours. Out with it."

She shook her head. "It's probably nothing, Nate. I just have an uneasy feeling about these fires. I don't know what it is, but something isn't right."

The next day she walked into town to see Lily. The wind was a little brisk, but it was a good day for a walk, with time to ponder. She found Lily in good spirits.

"Sister," she said, "I've been through a lot worse than this. A house can be fixed. Besides, I have plenty of company at the boarding house. I like Mary, and Sarah makes everyone happy."

Lily's good spirits soon wore off on Carrie, and she left to go visit Belinda with an improved state of mind. She arrived to find Belinda, Nettie, and Mary all working in the dress shop, chatting away as they worked. Nellie was telling a story that made the other two laugh.

Belinda looked up from her sewing. "Why, Maw, it's good to see you in town. Is everything okay?"

"Yes," responded Carrie. "I just came to check on Lily, but she is calm and happy."

"It was a bad thing," said Nettie, "but it could have been so much worse."

"It certainly could have," agreed Mary, continuing on with her needlework.

"Have you heard what caused the fire?" asked Carrie.

"No, not a thing," answered Belinda. "In a kitchen it could be anything."

Carrie made no response, but withdrew into her thoughts. The girls went back to their chatter.

"Mrs. Walsh will be by for her new dress this afternoon," said Mary.

"Yes, and she'll find some fault with it, I guarantee you," added Nettie.

"Now girls, be kind," admonished Belinda. "She just complains, and then goes on. Then we usually see her proudly wearing the dress on Sunday, telling everyone what a terrific job we did. It's just her way. Right, Maw?"

Carrie didn't answer, lost in thought.

"Maw, are you still with us?" asked Belinda, smiling.

"Oh? Oh, yes, Dear," Carrie spluttered. "I guess I was just thinking. For some reason, these fires have me worried."

"Worried?" asked Mary, a question in her eyes.

"Maybe it just makes you think about the loss of the barn," offered Nettie. "Sometimes it takes a while to get over things like that. I remember once when lightning hit our little shed out back. After that, lightning just scared me to death for a long time."

"I'm sure that's it," replied Carrie. "Well, girls, I'd better be getting on home. Nate will wonder what's happened to me. I hope to see all of you at church Sunday, and come to Sunday dinner afterwards. That includes the two of you, Mary and Nettie."

"Grandma Carrie!" called a young voice from the foyer. "Grandma Carrie, are you here?"

About that time Jacob, Luke's youngest, burst through the doorway, followed by his dad.

"Grandma Carrie, we have you a letter!" cried Jacob excitedly. Jacob Troy, Luke's seven-year-old, had been named for Troy Aston, once sheriff of Haymaker, who held a special place in Luke's heart. He had helped Luke get away from his abusive father, and had given him his first job. Later he had done the same for Jessie, eventually training him for the sheriff's job. Troy was the one who had found Tom that day...

"A letter!" laughed Carrie, as she gave her grandson a big hug. "I sure do like the new mailman Haymaker has sent to me."

Luke shook his head, trying to hide a smile. "Miss Ocie brought the letter over from the post office. She saw that it was from Ohio, and thought it might be important. Jacob had seen you come into the hotel, so we decided we would deliver it."

"From Ohio..." Carrie looked at the return address. "Why, it's from my brother Charles. I hope nothing is wrong." Her two brothers, Charles and Sile J., had moved with their families to Ohio several years ago to find work in the factories. Two years ago Lula, Sile J.'s wife, had passed away. It still brought a tear to Carrie's eye to think about it. Sile J. and Lula had lived with Papa Silas and lovingly cared for him after Mama Cynth died. Then their little boy, Woody, and Papa Silas had died on the same day, of complications from measles. Lula had never really recovered from the loss of little Woody. God had given her another son and daughter, but one child never replaces another.

As Carrie sat looking at the letter, Mary asked, "Miss Carrie, how many brothers do you have?"

Carrie's face took on a sudden sadness. "There were four of them. Will and his wife Sally moved to Kentucky a few years back. Eb, my oldest brother, passed away about seven years ago after a fall from their barn roof, and his wife Maggie followed only a few months later. Their children are scattered in different states. I haven't seen any of them in years. It's been at least three years since I've seen Charles or Sile J. I wonder..."

"Maw, why don't you just open it so you won't worry?" suggested Belinda.

Without another word, Carrie tore open the letter and began to read silently. The others waited patiently. Carrie's face suddenly broke into a smile and her eyes took on a sparkle.

"They're moving back!" she squealed. "My brothers are moving back! Listen to this..."

"Dear Sister,

"I hope this finds you and all your family well. It seems like ages since we've talked, and we all miss you. I have news which I hope will please you. Sile J. has not done well since Lula died and has been unable to work for about a year now. None of us are young anymore. Therefore, we have decided to move back to Haymaker. Our children will remain here, as they have good jobs and have raised their families here. Sile J., Lucinda and I will be coming home in about two weeks. We are hoping to live in the old homeplace, if it is still empty and livable. I must ask a favor of you. Would you check out the house and let us know if it is still in condition for three of us to live in? If it is, would you open the windows and let it air out a bit. If not, let us know. If I don't hear from you in a week, I will assume things are in condition for us to move back. I look forward to coming home."

"Oh, that's wonderful," said Belinda, with a heartfelt sigh.

"I always liked our uncles," agreed Luke. "It will be good to have them back, and maybe it will be good for Sile J. I'm looking forward to Mary Alice and Jacob getting to know them."

Carrie rose quickly. "I must hurry home. I can't wait to tell Nate! I'm sure the house is still in decent shape, but we'll go over tomorrow to check on it. We can clean it up and air it out for them."

Belinda and Luke looked at each other as if to say, *That's our mother!*

After giving hugs she took her leave, smiling as she walked quickly toward home. Before long, she was humming.

Nate was just as thrilled as Carrie, and the next day they headed over the hill in their old wagon to the little house where she had grown up, with buckets, cleaning cloths, and a broom. As they topped the hill, Carrie's heart filled with memories. She had enjoyed a wonderful childhood, and the sight of her old home brought tears to her eyes. Oh, how she missed Mama and Papa.

"It still looks good from here," said Nate, trying to draw her from the sad thoughts he could see in her face.

Carrie smiled weakly. "It brings back so many memories, Nate, but they are good memories. Don't worry, I won't be sad today. We have work to do, and my brothers are coming home!"

They found the inside of the house in excellent condition for one that had stood empty for so long. Dust was thick, but sheets had covered much of the furniture to keep it clean. They removed those, took them outside to shake them, and began the dusting. As they worked, Carrie entertained Nate with childhood stories.

"See the old sycamore tree, Nate? I was afraid it had rotted down, but it's still there! I remember when Papa found the little bird lying under it that Charles had killed with his sling shot. Papa didn't get angry or spank Charles, but he told him how much God loves the birds. Poor Charles felt so awful. I can assure you he never killed another bird!"

Carrie pulled a sheet from a rocking chair worn with age, and once again the tears came. "Papa's rocking chair," she sighed. "I can see him so clearly, sitting here early in the morning and sometimes late at night, reading his Bible. I sat on his lap here many times and looked into his face as he told a story, totally captured by the scenes he created with his words. I thought he was the grandest papa in the whole world. He was sitting in this rocker beside Mama's bed when she died, one hand on her Bible and one hand in his."

She turned from the rocking chair to get on with her work. While Carrie swept the floors, Nate went to check the barn and other outbuildings. It was late afternoon before they started home, and they were grateful Carrie had packed the picnic lunch they had shared earlier. Nate was already hungry for supper. It had been a good day, and the little house was ready for its new residents. They topped the hill once more, this time to look down upon their own house. It was a welcoming sight, but just as they got halfway down the hill, they heard a siren.

"Oh, no!" cried Carrie. "It's the fire siren!"

Nate took her hand. "What can it be this time?" he asked, almost to himself.

"Something's not right, Nate," Carrie said in a sad voice. "Mark my words, something is not right."

CHAPTER 9

While Nate milked the cow and fed the other animals, Carrie fixed supper. Her thoughts were far from what she was doing. First their barn, then Lily's house...something wasn't right. She just had a feeling in her bones.

They ate in apprehensive silence, hoping someone would come by soon to tell them what had been on fire.

"You know, Carrie," said Nate, breaking the silence, "we need to think about getting a telephone. We're not getting any younger, and we might need to call for help sometime. We could get in touch with the children quickly that way. Why don't we talk to them about it this Sunday? They will know what steps we need to take, and it will be well worth the money. What do you think?"

"I like the idea," answered Carrie, her forehead wrinkled. "I wish we had one right now."

They finished supper and were doing the dishes together, as they often did, when the front door opened.

"Maw! Nate!" It was Jessie's voice.

"In the kitchen!" called Carrie.

At the first sight of Jessie's face, she knew the news wasn't good. "What is it, son? The fire?"

He simply nodded his head. "It was the mercantile, Maw."

Carrie clutched the chair with one hand and her racing heart with the other. "Anyone..."

"No! No!" Jessie responded quickly, taking her arm. "No, Maw, no one was hurt. The mercantile wasn't even damaged too badly. They caught the fire in time. It was mostly the storage rooms in the back. They were completely destroyed, along with all the merchandise back there. One wall of the mercantile was blackened, and there's some smoke damage. The store will have to remain closed for a week or two. Thank God it didn't get to the rooms upstairs, although the smell of smoke makes them unlivable right now. No one was home at the time except Syrena. She was working downstairs in the store and smelled the smoke. Luke had gone on delivery."

"Praise God!" gasped Carrie, collapsing in a chair. "Jessie, what is going on? This can't just be a series of accidents. I didn't think too much about it when the barn burned, but when Lily's house caught on fire I just had this feeling..."

Jessie took a chair next to his mother and Nate sat down across from them. "Jessie, what is going on? Do you know something about the fires? I saw some questions in your eyes the day we went out to look over the barn."

"Yes, Papa Nate," he responded, "even then, I saw something to arouse suspicion. There was a strong smell of kerosene, and I found the remnants of a rag reeking of the same smell. The same was true of the fire at Lily's. I haven't been able to examine the storerooms yet because of the heat and smoldering, but I'm going back and check tonight. I have a feeling I will find the same source of the fire."

"But who would do these things, son?" asked Nate. "Is it just a coincidence that it has happened to our family, or is it someone who has targeted us?"

Jessie shook his head. "I just don't know yet, Papa, but I intend to find out."

"Jessie, your Maw and I have just been talking. We would like to have a telephone put in, and now I feel even more strongly about it. Can you help us?"

"Absolutely!" Jessie nodded his head. "I think that would be wise. I'll get the ball rolling first thing tomorrow."

He took his leave and headed back to the mercantile, and Carrie and Nate sat for a long time in silence. Who could be doing this? Did they have enemies they knew nothing about?

The following day, after a restless sleep for both, Carrie and Nate headed into town. They went straight to the mercantile. Carrie's eyes filled with tears as she smelled the smoke and saw the merchandise and furniture that had been moved outside. Several people were helping Luke empty the building.

"Hi Maw! Hi Nate!" Luke called cheerfully, setting down an armload of goods. "Looks like we've got ourselves a mess, doesn't it?"

"Yes, it does," answered Nate, following Luke's lighthearted manner. "Tell me what I can do, Son. I'm here to help."

Luke nodded. "All help is appreciated. Just grab anything you see inside, and move it out here on the porch. It all needs to be aired out."

"Where are Syrena and the kids?" asked Carrie.

"Syrena is upstairs, cleaning and airing out the place. The kids are in school. We decided to keep things as normal as possible for them."

Carrie nodded. "That's a good idea. Where are you staying, Luke? You are all welcome to stay with us, you know."

Giving her a kiss on the cheek, he replied, "Thanks, Maw. You're the best, but we lucked up; we're staying in Lily's house. It was finished just the day before our fire."

"Oh, that's wonderful," replied Carrie. "That was fast work."

"As it turned out," said Luke, "about ten men from the town, Floyd acting as leader, pitched in and made fast work of the repairs. Lily sent word for us to move in as soon as she heard about our fire. Can't tell you how much that means to us."

Carrie patted Luke's arm. "I'll leave you to your work, but I'll be back to help. I'm going over to the boarding house to see Lily, and then on to the hotel for a few minutes."

She took her leave and headed toward the boarding house. As she entered, Sarah McLindy greeted her.

"Why, 'tis good to see you, Carrie! I'm so sorry about that nasty fire, but thankful to the good Lord that no one was hurt. Things can be replaced, but not our loved ones."

Carrie gave Sarah a hug. Mother McLindy, as most people of the town called her, was the most positive person she had ever met.

"I am very thankful that Luke and his family are well," Carrie replied. "Our God is so good."

"That He is. That He is," avowed Sarah, bustling along with her work as she talked.

"Is Lily here?" asked Carrie.

"I most definitely am," laughed Lily, coming down the stairs. "It's good to see you, Sister."

"And it's good to see you, Lily," said Carrie. "I wanted to thank you for letting Luke and Syrena borrow your house. I'm sorry it will delay your moving back."

"Oh, I'm not moving back," responded Lily, with a *we have a secret* look at Sarah.

Carrie looked perplexed. "You're not moving back?"

"Nope! I'm not moving back."

Carrie had that *what are you up to* look on her face that she used to have when they were girls, and Lily was being naughty. Lily had to laugh.

"I'm staying right here," she said.

"Okay, Lily, enough with the drama," warned Carrie. "If Papa Silas was here I would sic him on you."

Sarah McLindy laughed at the looks on the two sisters' faces. One was having a good time confusing the other, and the other was exasperated with her sibling.

"Lily," she admonished, "don't confuse your sister. Out with it!"

"Come sit down, Carrie," said Lily, motioning toward the cozy little sitting area.

When the three of them were seated, she continued. "I like it here, with Sarah and Mary, and the others who come and go. There's life here! My little house had become a weathered tomb. Sarah has made a proposal, and I have accepted. First of all, I'm selling my house to Luke and Syrena, if they choose to buy it. We talked a little about it the other day, even before the mercantile caught fire. I told them last night to move in and take their time in deciding."

"That was so thoughtful of you, Lily," said Carrie, wiping away a tear.

Lily continued, "I am going to become partners with Sarah in owning and operating the boarding house."

"I'm not as young as I once was," inserted Sarah, winking. "Though I wouldn't want the word to get out. I've been thinking for a while now that I might have to give up my boarding house, and the idea broke my heart. Then God sent Lily here, although under dreadful circumstances. 'The Lord moves in mysterious ways,' the Reverend always said."

Sarah still referred to her husband, a deceased minister, as the Reverend.

"What about your job at the orphanage?" asked Carrie, trying to get the matter straight in her mind.

"They have enough help there," replied Lily. "Mary Carlisle is a good worker, and an excellent cook. Then there's Matthew and Anja to help. Mary is teaching Anja to cook. Martha, Luke, and John can help, for now. Of course, Floyd is there...and I think they are going to hire Nettie's niece, Alma, to help part time. They will be fine."

Before she could think about her words, Carrie asked, "But what about you and Floyd?"

Lily gave that "Lily laugh"; Carrie had missed hearing it. "Oh, Sister, you are a matchmaker."

Carrie blushed from head to toe. "I'm sorry. That was a nosy thing to say."

"No, no," laughed Lily, obviously enjoying her sister's red face. "I like Floyd, and I enjoy his company—but I won't marry again, and he knows that. I don't think he wants to marry, either. We like things just the way they are, and I'm looking forward to this next step in my life. I'm the happiest I've been since my Dent died. I've done a lot of bad things in my life, Carrie, but God has forgiven me, and so have you. And so did Alice, before she died. Now I want to give to others, make friends and just enjoy this life God has given me."

Carrie reached for Lily's hand. "I am so happy for you, Lily, and so proud of you. I forgave you long ago, and I love you, Sister Dear."

Tears made happy trickles down Sarah McLindy's face as she watched the two sisters. "With God all things are possible," she said. "The Reverend believed that with all his heart."

Carrie, her heart a little lighter, left the two happy friends to go on to the hotel. There she found Belinda dusting the furniture in the foyer. She looked up from her work with a bright smile.

"Good morning, Maw!" she greeted her mother. "I guess I know what brings you into town. Where's Nate?"

Carrie gave her oldest daughter a hug. "He's at the mercantile helping Luke. I just came from the boarding house. I learned all kinds of new things."

She proceeded to tell Belinda about Lily's and Sarah's news, and Luke's pending decision about the house.

Belinda smiled. "It always amazes me how God can bring good things out of bad."

"How is your shop going?" asked Carrie, changing the subject.

"I have more work than I can handle," answered Belinda. "I don't know what I would do without Nettie and Mary. Cammy is becoming quite a good helper, too."

"That's wonderful," said Carrie. "I think that is Cammy's niche in life. Before we know it she will be starting her millinery."

"I think you're right," nodded Belinda.

"I'm glad Mary moved here," said Carrie. "She's been a help to a lot of people, and Lily and Sarah seem to enjoy having her at the boarding house."

Belinda spoke as she continued dusting. "She is an amazing woman, talented in so many ways...and yet there's a sadness about her. I can't explain it, but I'm hoping as she continues to live and work here, we can help dispel that sadness."

"Will you be coming to dinner Sunday?" asked Carrie, as she rose to leave.

"As far as I know," answered Belinda. "Christopher is home today with a fever and sore throat, but I'm sure he'll probably be better by then. You know how these things are with kids."

On Sunday, Carrie and Nate rode to church with Ady Rose and her family. It felt good to go to church after a troublesome week. Homer and Trula seemed so happy after years of worry and heartbreak. She and Nate needed to talk to them after church, and she prayed it would go well. Matthew and Anja were there, and Anja was glowing in a way only expectant mothers are able to do. The rest of Homer's family seemed happier, too, with smiling faces as they talked to the other young people, something they hadn't done in a long time. It was good to see them all heal. Lily was there, sitting between Sarah McLindy and Floyd. Cindy and Landon were there with the twins, each proudly carrying one of their sons.

"Good morning, my brothers and sisters," said Homer, stepping to the pulpit. "It is a bright sunny day, and we are in the house of the Lord. What more could we ask for? Let's lift up our voices to God as we sing number 143, 'What a Friend We Have in Jesus.'"

The little congregation began to sing with exuberance. At the end of the song, Homer led them in prayer and everyone was seated.

Homer waited for quiet. "This is a special day for many reasons. First, we have Mr. Daniel Landon McLindy and Mr. David Charles McLindy here with us for the very first time. Congratulations to you, Landon and Cindy. You are starting those boys off right. I remember what it was like to get one baby ready on Sunday morning...and I remember what it was like to get *five* little ones ready."

Everyone laughed in response.

Homer continued. "I am also glad that Luke Swank and his family are here today. We are sorry for your loss in the fire, but we praise God that no one was hurt."

This was followed by a chorus of "amens!"

"There is one more thing we want to share before we get down to the sermon. As you know, our daughter Lissa, whom God gave to us at the age of twelve, has been searching for her birth parents with our blessing. Lissa, come tell the folks your news."

Nathan and Lissa walked to the front. "I want to thank all of you for your good wishes and prayers in my search for my birth parents. We did have some results this week. I learned who my birth mother was, and that she died two weeks after I was born. She didn't just give me away, and that means a lot to me. Her name was Anna. I'm sad that I will never know her, but God knows what is best. I also found out who my father is, but that is not as pleasant to tell. You see, my father is in prison. He and my mother were married, and from what I've been told, they were happy together. When she died, something seemed to happen to him. There had been an accident, causing my mother to go into labor; when she died, my father blamed the man who caused the accident. He killed that man, and that's why he's in prison. I hope to someday meet my father, but in the meantime, I ask all of you to pray for him. Our God is a God of mercy and forgiveness, and we are to be the same."

Nathan and Lissa returned to their seats, and the church was silent. Then Eli Barns spoke. "What better time is there to pray for him, Brother Homer, than right now?"

Eli then led the church in a prayer for Lissa's father, as heads bowed and tears flowed.

After church, Carrie and Nate greeted neighbors and friends and waited to talk to Homer and Trula. When everyone had taken their leave, the four of them walked back into the church. Nate began without hesitation, for he knew they had family coming for dinner, as did he and Carrie.

"Homer, I hope I'm not sticking my nose in where I shouldn't, and if I am I apologize. I know how much your son Luke loves horses, and I know it his dream to work with them. As you know, our son Clay and his wife Abigail own a horse ranch in Kentucky."

Homer and Trula looked at each other. Nate couldn't tell just what the look meant, so he continued.

"I have not spoken to your Luke about this, because I wanted to see what you think first. We have talked with Clay. He would like to have Luke come work for him on the ranch."

He paused to let them speak.

"Oh, my," Homer finally said. "I don't know what to say. This is quite a surprise."

Nate looked doubtful. "I'm sorry if I have done something I shouldn't, but Luke doesn't have to know if you are against this."

"No, no," Homer said quickly. "We are not against this at all. Trula and I have wondered how to help him with this dream of his. No, Nate, we are grateful to you for caring about our boy enough to look into this. Right, Trula?"

Trula finally smiled. "No mother wants to see her child leave, Nate, but every mother wants to see her child happy. This will be a dream come true for Luke."

"Will there be a place for him to stay?" asked Homer. "Will he be able to earn his keep?"

"Clay has a large bunkhouse," answered Nate. "It's a really nice bunkhouse, where all of his hired hands stay. The pay is excellent for a young man starting out, and his board and meals will be free. I don't know all the details, but Clay is coming home in two weeks, and with your permission, he would like to talk to Luke and the two of you."

"That will be perfect," said Homer, grabbing Nate's hand and pumping it with vigor. "I can't tell you how much we appreciate this. We will go ahead and talk to Luke tonight, and prepare him for Clay's visit. I have an idea we will have one happy son. Thank you...both of you."

After more hugs and handshakes, Carrie and Nate took their leave, happy their idea had been well received. As they left the church, they saw Willy was waiting to drive them home.

"The others went on to get dinner started, Maw Carrie," he said.

When they arrived home, the girls were putting the finishing touches on the meal as Cammy and Mary Alice set the table. Carrie quickly removed her hat and donned her apron.

"Looks like you girls have everything under control," she said, "and my granddaughters have done a fine job of setting the table." The two girls beamed at their grandmother's praise.

As they finished getting the meal ready, Carrie filled them in on their conversation with Homer and Trula.

"Oh, Grandma Carrie," said Cammy, "that is just wonderful. I've never known anyone who loved horses more than Luke. I've seen his drawings, and you just wouldn't believe how good they are."

Carrie looked confused. "Drawings? What drawings?"

"Didn't you know?" asked Cammy. "He has oodles and oodles of horse pictures, and he's quite the artist."

"No," replied Carrie, "I didn't know, but I guess I shouldn't be surprised. Clay loved horses as much if not more than Luke, and he drew pictures of them all the time. His room was lined with his drawings."

The meal was soon ready, and the men and children were called. As they ate, they discussed all the happenings in the family and the little town. Eventually the fires were brought up.

"What about the mercantile fire, Jessie?" asked Carrie. "Did you find any evidence of the cause?"

63

Taking a drink of tea, Jessie said, "Yes, Maw, I'm afraid I did. Someone seems to be setting these fires. Now I have to find out who the culprit is. Right now, I have no idea. I've looked into newcomers in the town and neighborhood, and I've checked on youngsters, but so far nothing has panned out. I just hope we can find them soon, before they do more damage."

"But why is it just our family this is happening to?" asked Belinda. "What would anyone have against us?"

"That's what I want to know," chimed in Ady Rose. "I don't know of anything harmful we have done to anyone. If Paw was still alive I might understand it, but he's been dead for years."

"I don't know the answers, Sis," said Jessie, "but I will find out. I promise you that."

Changing the subject, Nate said, "I told the boys about the plans for Luke, Carrie."

She smiled. "And I told the girls, so I guess everyone knows. The added bonus to it all is that Clay will be coming home in less than two weeks."

"Homer's family has suffered so much," said Joe, Belinda's husband. "It's great to see good things finally happening to them."

A few hours later everyone took their leave, and Carrie and Nate were once more alone. It was a warm evening, so they sat on the porch in their rockers, and Nate held Carrie's hand. As they rocked, they talked about the day. While they were talking, they saw two men pull up to the gate at the bottom of the hill.

"That looks like Homer and Luke," said Nate.

The men walked up the hill. "Hope we're not paying a visit two late in the day," called Homer.

"Of course not, Homer," called Carrie. "Come on up. We're always glad to see you. Come have a seat."

"We talked everything over with Luke," said Homer, taking a seat, "and he wanted to come see you."

Luke sat down on the top step and turned to Carrie and Nate. "I couldn't wait another day to see you and thank you. This is a dream come true for me, and I'm indebted to you, Aunt Carrie and Uncle Nate. Thank you for caring enough about me to do this. I promise I will do a good job for Clay and make you proud of me."

Carrie patted his shoulder. "We once had a son who loved horses just like you do, Luke. It was hard to see him leave home, but we knew he had to follow his dream. Now he's the owner of a large horse ranch, has a family, and is happy, and he wants to help you follow your dream. It's a beautiful ranch in the flat part of Kentucky, and I know you're going to love it."

"We're just glad he'll be with family," said Homer. "Trula won't worry nearly as much, knowing he's being looked after."

"What's this I hear about you being an artist?" asked Carrie.

Luke turned a bright red, but his father replied. "You should see all of his drawings, Aunt Carrie. He has drawing books full of them! Horses standing alone, horses in the corral, horses running across the land... They are very, very good."

Luke, embarrassed, hung his head.

Carrie squeezed his shoulder. "Luke, listen to me. Don't be embarrassed. This is a gift you have, and gifts come from God. When He gives us a gift or talent, we are to use it. You keep drawing. Perhaps one day you can have a showing of them in a museum. It can happen, you know. Besides, I think you will find that you and your cousin have more than one thing in common."

"Thank you, Aunt Carrie," Luke answered. "I promise I'll use every talent God gives me. I guess I just never thought anyone would care about my drawings."

Soon Homer and Luke left for home, and Carrie and Nate leaned their heads back and just rocked.

"You know, some days are good," said Nate, "and other days are great."

The following week, the week before Easter, Carrie and Nate had their first telephone installed. True to his word, Jessie had worked everything out for them.

"You are on a party line with Harold and Nancy Moser," said the telephone man. "If the telephone rings once, it is for them. If it rings twice, it's for you." With these instructions, he took his leave.

Carrie and Nate stood and looked at the phone. "I guess we should call Jessie and thank him," said Nate. "Go ahead, Carrie."

Carrie looked at the phone with uncertainty.

"Go ahead," urged Nate, encouraging Carrie while keeping his distance from the ominous black device.

"Don't you want to be the first to use it?" asked Carrie with just a touch of pleading in her voice.

Nate shook his head. "Wouldn't think of it."

Reluctantly Carrie reached out to pick up the receiver. Her hand clutched it and then halted.

"Go ahead, Carrie," urged Nate. "You can do it."

Carrie noticed he wasn't getting any closer to it. Drawing a deep breath, she lifted the receiver.

"Operator! Number please!" said a shrill nasal voice.

Carrie almost dropped the phone.

"Operator! Number please!" said the shrill voice again.

"Uh...uh...this is Carrie Swank and I..."

"Why, hello, Carrie!" The shrill voice rose a bit higher. "This is Mertie Barns. Glad you finally got a phone! Now who do you want to call?"

"M-my son Jessie," squeaked Carrie, as Nate nodded his head in encouragement. "His number is 3550."

"Oh, I know his number!" shrilled Mertie. "One moment please!"

"I hear it ringing," Carrie whispered excitedly to Nate.

"Hello," said a woman's voice. "Amanda Swank speaking."

"Oh, Amanda," answered Carrie with relief. This is Maw Carrie. The man just finished installing our new phone and I wanted to call and thank Jessie for taking care of it for us."

"That's wonderful, Maw Carrie," responded Amanda. "Jessie's not here right now, but I'll have him call you the minute he gets home. What is your number?"

"Uh-uh...I don't know," said Carrie. "I forgot to ask the man. Nate, do you know our number?"

Nate shook his head.

"Your number is 3277!" said the shrill voice of Mertie Barns, seeming to feel no shame for listening to their conversation.

Amanda laughed. "I wrote it down, and I'll have Jessie call you. I'm glad you have a phone now, Maw Carrie...and thank you, Mertie!"

With this, there was silence. After pausing a moment Carrie put the receiver back in its place, feeling like she had just fought a battle.

"See," said Nate. "There was nothing to it."

About an hour later the phone rang twice. Carrie and Nate looked at each other.

"Did he say our ring was one or two?" asked Carrie.

CHAPTER 10

Easter arrived wrapped in warm temperatures and sunshine. Redbuds colored the hillsides, and daffodils and tulips brought their smiling hues to the yards and roadsides. It was a good day to go to church and then enjoy family. That was important in the little town of Haymaker and the Lacy Creek community. In fact, Easter was important all over the hills and valleys of the Appalachians. Carrie awoke with a cheery feeling dancing in her soul. She was happy: the happiest she could ever remember being. She looked at Nate, still sleeping beside her. *Thank you God*, she whispered in her heart. *This is a big reason for my happiness...Nate, my children...my grandchildren...my friends...I have so much to thank you for.*

As she lay there looking toward the window and the sunshine, memories poured in. There had been some bad Easters in her life, but most of them were filled with joyful memories. She remembered the ones of her childhood, with Mama and Papa. They had been so much fun. Charles and Eb were the best egg hiders in the world. She almost laughed out loud when she remembered the time Eb had hidden an Easter egg under Mama's old sitting hen. No one could find it, and finally Eb had to confess where he had hidden it. Mama scolded him but couldn't hide her laughter. Oh, what special days those were! *I miss Eb so much*, Carrie thought. *I'm glad Charles and Sile J. are coming home. Just one more thing to thank you for, God.*

Her reminiscing came to a halt as Nate awoke and turned toward her. "Good morning, my beautiful Easter bunny!" he said, leaning to give her a kiss.

"Good morning, my Nate," she answered. "It is the most beautiful morning I have ever seen."

"Then I guess we'd better get up and get started," said Nate. "We have a full day ahead of us."

A few hours later, with much of their Easter dinner prepared, the happy pair left for church. They arrived to see quite a crowd gathered. After lots of hugs, howdies, and handshaking, they settled in their pews for the service. Homer greeted the congregation, had prayer, and everyone sang "I Know that My Redeemer Lives." As the congregation sat once more an expectant quiet prevailed. As Sarah began to play, Mary Carlisle rose and walked to the front. Lily looked back at Carrie and smiled. Mary began to sing "I'd Rather Have Jesus." There was total silence as they listened to the words of the song, and her beautiful soprano voice. Nate reached for Carrie's hand, wanting to share this precious moment with her.

After the service, the people said their goodbyes, families heading out together to share this special day. Lily's family was having dinner at Homer's. Carrie's family would be with her and Nate. Just as they were getting in the car with Willy and Ady Rose, a truck pulled in and a voice called out, "We'll just follow you!"

Carrie turned and then gasped as her eyes lit up, "Oh, it's Clay!"

She ran to her baby boy, joy filling every step. "Oh, Clay, it's so good to see you. I didn't expect you until next week. Who is with you? Oh, this is wonderful!"

Logan, Clay's oldest son, emerged from the passenger's side and came toward them smiling.

"You look so much like your father," said Carrie, pulling him into a loving hug.

Logan returned the hug. "It's so good to see you, Grandma Carrie. Mother made us come to share Easter with you so we could be with all the family. She said we could share other Easters with her and my brother and sister."

"Your mother is wonderful and thoughtful," said Carrie. "You give her a big hug and 'thank you' for me."

What a wonderful day they had! Carrie had everyone of her children home once more, along with most of her grandchildren. They had so much to talk about. She and Nate just sat back, watched, listened and smiled. *This must be the closest thing I know to Heaven*, thought Carrie.

"Clay," said Jessie, "Are you still enjoying your horse ranch? You can always move back here, you know."

"Jessie, I would love to be closer to all of you, but I could never leave my horses. I love what I do. Logan is a big help, and he loves it as much as I do."

"Tell us about your other children," urged Ady Rose. "Do they love ranching?"

Clay smiled proudly. "Levi is nine now, and does like the ranch, but it's not his true love. Levi wants to be an architect. He loves creating things and is quite good at it, if you don't mind a papa boasting. He has designed several useful structures for the ranch, even at his young age. Lydia is six and it's a bit soon to say where her heart lies, but she does love the horses, and even at her age she is good with them. I just want my children to be happy, so I will support them in whatever career they choose, just like Maw did me. I know she didn't want me to go away, but she loved me enough to let me follow my dream." With this he leaned over and kissed his mother's hand.

"Is Luke going back with you?" asked Cammy.

"That is my hope," answered Clay. "I'm going to talk with him tomorrow. If he loves horses as much as I've heard, he will be a great asset to us."

"Did Grandma Carrie tell you about his drawings?" asked Cammy.

Clay looked at Carrie, a questioning expression on his face.

Carrie smiled. "Do you remember all the drawings you used to do of horses, Clay? From the time you were able to hold a pencil, you were drawing horses. You would tack each one on the wall and declare it your favorite. Well, Luke draws, too. I haven't seen them, but I'm told he has a talent."

"Oh, I've seen them," declared Cammy, "and they are fantastic."

"Well," said Clay, "it seems my cousin and I have more than one thing in common. I'm anxious to meet this young man."

Changing the subject, Belinda asked, "Maw, when are Charles and Sile J. supposed to get here?"

"Sometime this week," Carrie replied. "I'm not sure just which day. I'm hoping they will let me know, so some of us can meet the train. I'm really anxious to see my brothers again. We had such happy, fun-filled Easters when we were back at home. My brothers made sure we didn't have a dull moment."

She told them the story about Eb hiding the egg under the hen.

"Now there's an idea..." said Jessie, giving the youngsters a mischievous look.

"Don't you do it, Uncle Jessie," said Christopher.

This brought laughter from the others.

The rest of the day was filled with Easter egg hunts, games, and lots of chatter. It was late in the afternoon when the last ones left. Carrie, Nate, Clay, and Logan sat on the porch, watching them leave and loving the warm weather.

"So, Maw," said Clay, after a while, "tell me about these fires you've been having around here. Do you think someone is deliberately setting them?"

"It seems that way," answered Carrie. "The thing I don't understand is why it is happening only to our family."

"Could it be a coincidence?" asked Clay.

"It's possible," said Nate. "We just hope they're over."

"I think after breakfast tomorrow Logan and I will go by to see Homer, Trula, and Luke," said Clay. "I want to get to know him and make sure he plans to go back to Kentucky with us, and I want to assure his parents that Abigail and I will take care of him. I also want to see the horse drawings Cammy talked about."

The next day Clay and Logan left to go into Haymaker while Carrie and Nate stayed home to clean up after a busy Easter Sunday. About midmorning the telephone rang. Carrie answered, feeling much more at ease with their new mechanism.

"Hello!"

"Carrie?" inquired a male voice.

"Yes, this is Carrie."

"Well, this is your brother," laughed the voice. "This is Charles. I just wanted to let you know we will be arriving this Wednesday."

"Oh, Charles, that's wonderful!" said Carrie. "I can't wait to see all of you. The house is in good shape and ready for you. I'll have one of the boys meet you at the train station."

"Thank you, Carrie," he said. "We are looking forward to seeing all of you, and catching up on the years."

As she hung up the receiver, Carrie felt a warm glow in her heart. She had enjoyed an Easter with all her children, and now her brothers would soon be home. She could not remember feeling such joy and peace—except for those fires.

Clay returned from visiting with Homer, Trula and Luke. He felt a kinship with Luke already, and was anxious to take him back to Kentucky with him.

"He reminds me so much of myself at that age, Maw," he said. "He has that true love for horses. I saw his drawings, too. I have some ideas about that, but I won't talk about them just yet. It's just an idea brewing in my head."

The day ended all too soon, and the following morning Carrie and Nate said goodbye to Clay and Logan, with a promise from Clay to come back soon. Carrie felt a loss at their leaving, but the happiness overshadowed it. Clay was where he was happy, and soon Luke would be also. God had a plan for each of them. After they left, Carrie lit in to her cleaning and cooking. She was planning a "welcome home" meal for Charles, Lucinda, and Sile J., plus food to take home with them. Lucinda would have her hands full the next few days just getting settled in, and would have little time for cooking. She was on her way to the smokehouse to get a ham for the occasion when she smelled smoke. Her heart did a leap.

"Nate!" she called. "Nate, where are you?"

Just then he came out of the barn. "I smell it!" He called. "Where is it coming from?"

They looked in all directions. "Oh no!" exclaimed Carrie. "Nate, it's coming from the homeplace. Oh, dear God, don't let Mama and Papa's house be on fire!"

"I'll hitch up the wagon," said Nate. "You call Jessie."

Within minutes, they were headed across the hill. When they reached the top they saw the fire.

"Look, Carrie!" cried Nate. "It's not the house! Praise God, it's not the house!"

Carrie began to weep from sheer relief. It was the barn! She never thought she would feel happy to see a barn burning, but she was over-joyed that it was not the house. They sat for a moment watching the fire, knowing it was too late to save the barn.

"Another fire," said Carrie. "I had hoped there would be no more. What a terrible welcome home for my brothers."

"At least they have their house," soothed Nate. "They have a home to stay in. The barn can be rebuilt."

From their place on the hilltop they saw Jessie's car pull in at the homeplace, so they called to the horses and headed on down. As Jessie stopped the car, they could see that Luke was with him. The boys stood and watched the barn burn, turning only when Carrie and Nate pulled up.

"We didn't call the fire brigade, Maw," said Jessie. "It was too far out here for them to do any good."

Carrie nodded. "I was so hoping the fires had ended."

"Nate, why don't you and Maw go back home?" suggested Luke. "None of us can do anything right now. We'll stay to make sure the fire doesn't get out or get to the house. Jessie probably can't inspect it before tonight or tomorrow."

Taking Luke's advice, they headed back across the hill. Carrie had much to do before her brothers arrived. She just dreaded giving them bad news on their first day back.

CHAPTER 11

Carrie and Nate arrived at the train depot bright and early the next day with their farm wagon. Jessie was going to meet the newcomers with his car to drive them to Carrie's, but they could haul anything they brought with them in the wagon. The train pulled in at exactly 9:45. Carrie could hardly contain her excitement, but when Sile J. stepped from the train she hardly recognized him. He had aged unbelievably. His hair was white as the winter snow, and he had lost weight. His face was lean and drawn. Behind him, Lucinda stepped down carefully. She had aged also, but she was still a lovely woman. There was gray in her hair, but her face was still young, with the softness Carrie remembered. Charles stepped down next, and it was like time had stood still. He was older, but he still had that impish youth about him. His eyes twinkled as he waved to them, and Carrie laughed just to look at him.

"We're here!" he called, his face jubilant. He said something to the porter before stepping to the ground, and Carrie saw him hand the man some money.

Dear, thoughtful Charles, she thought.

Carrie moved toward them and then there were hugs all around. As she hugged Sile J. she felt his thinness. "Sile J., it is so good to have you home."

He smiled a weak, sad smile. "I wish Lula could be with us," he said, a tear meandering down his gaunt face.

"And so do I, brother," she replied. "So do I."

Jessie arrived just then. The luggage was loaded into the wagon, while her brothers and Lucinda rode in Jessie's car. "Maw has one of her good meals fixed for you," he told them. "Then I'll drive you on to the home-place. I'm sorry to tell you, folks, but your barn burned yesterday."

"Oh, no," gasped Lucinda. "How did it catch fire?"

"I'm not sure," answered Jessie. "I'm going to look it over when we get there. Several fires have occurred around here lately, and we think someone is setting them. We just don't know who yet. Maybe some young-sters pulling pranks. We just don't know, but I intend to find out. Your house is fine, though. Maw and Papa Nate cleaned it up for you, and it's in good shape."

"You called him Papa Nate," said Charles. "I take it you are happy with your maw's marriage. She seems very happy."

Jessie smiled. "Nate is the finest man in the world, and the father we never had. He loves all of us like his own, but best of all, he loves our mother. No one could be better to her, and yes, she is the happiest she has ever been."

"I'm glad to hear that," replied Charles. "It's hard to imagine brothers being as different as Nate and Tom. Carrie deserves all the happiness life has to offer. I always tried to like Tom, but he made it mighty hard. He used to flirt with every woman he was around like he was cock-of-the-walk. He had to be noticed. I guess he just had the ole devil in him. Too bad. He had everything a man could want, and just never appreciated it. But I shouldn't be saying these things to you, Jessie. After all, he was your paw."

"Only by blood," muttered Jessie, an old bitterness creeping into his voice.

By this time, they had pulled in at the bottom of the hill below Carrie's and Nate's. They all disembarked and began the climb up the hill, stopping to look around every now and then and remark about changes since they had moved away.

"I remember watching the train stop here at the big tank and fill up with water as a boy," said Charles. "No matter how often I saw it, I was always mesmerized."

Carrie laughed. "I always liked waving at the man in the red caboose, and he never failed to wave back."

"Some of us boys use to stand on the rails when we knew the train was coming," said Sile J. "When we felt the vibration, we would bet on how long it would take the train to get to where we were."

Carrie and Charles looked at each other, surprised but glad to hear Sile J. take part in their conversation. Maybe moving back would be good for him.

At lunch they filled Carrie and Nate in on their families and the happenings during their years away, though Sile J. talked very little. Orin Tate and Ellen, Sile J.'s children, now had children of their own; Orin Tate even had five grandchildren. Charles' and Amanda's only child, Katherine, now had four children of her own.

"She made up for the ones we couldn't have," laughed Charles. "They're all girls, and all teenagers! I must say, they have brought us a lot of joy—and their parents some headaches! It was hard to leave them."

After the meal, the men went out to sit on the porch while Carrie and Lucinda did the dishes. It gave them all a chance to talk.

"Sile J. doesn't seem to be doing well, Lucinda," Carrie said.

Lucinda shook her head in acknowledgement. "No, he isn't. He's the main reason we moved back here. When Lula died, he just stopped living. He just sits most of the time. He doesn't even enjoy his grandchildren anymore, and they were once the apple of his eye. We just don't know what to do for him, so we thought moving back to the homeplace might spark some life into him. He talked about it quite often, with that far-away look in his eyes."

"He always adored Lula," said Carrie, "and she adored him. I remember when they first began courting. He was so nervous. Lula said everytime he came to her house he was like a Brahma bull in a chicken coop. He tried to do everything right, but ended up doing everything wrong. Her parents thought highly of him, though."

Lucinda laughed. "You know, he still treated her like a rare jewel. You should have seen the way he took care of her during her illness. He seldom left her bedside."

"I know a good way to start Sile J. on the road back to life," said Carrie.

"How?"

"Bring him to church Sunday," answered Carrie. "Do you think he'll come?"

"I don't know," replied Lucinda, "but you are right. He needs God right now more than anything. I think he's angry with God. We'll see what we can do."

Soon the dishes were finished and Sile J., Charles, and Lucinda headed out with Jessie, loaded down with enough food to do them several days. Carrie and Nate promised to check on them in a day or two to see how they were doing. In the meantime, Carrie had promised Belinda she would help her with some sewing for a wedding. It was keeping Mary and Nettie busy just doing the regular sewing. The next day she headed into town early in the morning, leaving Nate at home to do the chores. It was nice enough weather for her to walk, and walking always gave her time to think. Her mind went to the fires.

It's kind of strange, she thought to herself, *but the fires, as awful as they are, have never done any real damage. It's like the person setting them is just trying to cause aggravation. I wonder if Jessie has noticed that.*

She made herself a mental note to talk to him about it. Today, though, her mind would have to be on sewing and helping Belinda.

"I'm here!" she called, opening the hotel door.

"Hi, Grandma Carrie," called Christopher, bounding in to the foyer. Right behind him was Benjamin, Jessie's oldest.

"Hi, boys!" answered Carrie. "Benjamin, what are you doing here?"

"I just came by to walk to school with Christopher," he replied. "We're best buddies, you know."

Carrie laughed. "No, I didn't know, but I'm very glad. It's wonderful to be cousins *and* best buddies."

With this the boys were out the door just as Belinda appeared.

"Maw, I'm glad you are here. We have so much work to get done. I'm thankful for the business, but at times like this I get kind of nervous."

"Oh, we'll get it done," said Carrie, reassuringly. "We always do. Have you thought of hiring some part-time help?"

"Yes," answered Belinda. "I just don't know who it would be. Not everyone can do sewing like this, and those who can have families to take care of. Ady Rose is doing some sewing at home for me, so Mary can help us today. I almost have the bridal gown finished, but we still have the veil and four bridesmaid's dresses to make, and only two weeks to get them ready."

"We will get them done in plenty of time," said Mary Carlisle, entering the room. "Martha is filling in for me at the orphanage for the next few days, so I have plenty of time. It's good to see you, Miss Carrie."

"And good to see you," replied Carrie. She was amazed at the change in Mary, from a woman of shyness to one quite outgoing. She had filled out a little, too, making her cheeks a bit rosier. *She's actually a lovely young woman*, thought Carrie, as Mary was seated.

They set right in to the work. Nettie came about an hour after Carrie, and joined them as she worked on a new shirt for Berns Webb. They chatted like magpies as they worked. Carrie decided to be brave and ask Mary a few questions.

"Mary, you said you went to live at the orphanage at the age of eight, when your mother died. Do you mind me asking what she died of?"

Mary kept sewing.

"I'm sorry," said Carrie, after a moment. "I didn't mean to get too personal."

"She died of a broken neck."

"What?"

"She died of a broken neck."

Mary's eyes grew hard and Carrie could see the anger returning.

"Oh, my," gasped Carrie. "It must have been a terrible accident. Is it too hard to talk about it?"

"It wasn't an accident."

"Not an accident?"

The room was filled with a laden silence as needles ceased their in and out motion and all eyes turned to Mary. They waited.

Finally, Mary spoke again. "It wasn't an accident. My stepfather killed her."

"Oh, dear God!" exclaimed Nettie.

"I'm sorry, Mary," said Carrie. "I shouldn't have brought this up. It must be agonizing for you to even remember. Let's just talk about something else."

"Might as well get it out," said Mary, in a bitter tone. "He was the meanest man I ever knew. He drank, and that made him meaner—although he was mean enough when he was sober. He beat my mother almost daily, and when he got tired of hitting her, he started in on me."

"Couldn't your mother leave him?" asked Belinda, almost in a whisper.

"Oh, she tried. She tried several times, but he always found her, and then things were twice as bad. Then one day, he was totally out of control—and he broke her neck just like he was breaking a chicken bone. As easily and quickly as that, he took my mother from me. He fled from the house, leaving me alone there with her. It was at night, and we lived two miles from the nearest house."

"What did you do?" asked Nettie. "It must have been awful for someone just eight years old."

"I didn't do anything until morning," said Mary, in a matter-of-fact voice. "I simply lay on the floor beside her until daylight, and then I went to Mr. Wyling's house and told him and his wife what had happened. Mr. Wyling went for the sheriff, and I waited with Mrs. Wyling. She made me some breakfast and, surprisingly, I ate."

"Did they find him?"

"Yes, later that day they found him in the woods, passed out. He never showed one dab of remorse. They took him away and I never saw him again, thank God. He confessed to what he had done, and I didn't have to testify in court. As far as I know he is still in prison, and will be the rest of his life. I stayed on with Mr. and Mrs. Wyling until the state moved me to the orphanage. They were really kind to me."

"Were the people at the orphanage good to you?" asked Nettie.

"They weren't mean. They just didn't have time to show a lot of love like the children receive at Alice's Hope. We had to work pretty hard, but at least I didn't have to watch my mother being beaten or fear for my own life. I hated that man every day my mother was married to him, and truth be told, I still hate him."

"What about your real father, Mary?" asked Belinda. "Do you remember him?"

For a moment Mary's face paled. Then she smiled, and as she did so, she became a completely different person. "Oh, yes. I was only five when Papa died, but I remember."

Mary stopped speaking as though she was seeing something in the past. Then she continued, "Papa was the kindest man you could ever imagine. I remember sitting in his lap and looking into his face. His face was always filled with love, and we laughed together and played games together."

"What did he die of?" asked Nettie.

"Heart trouble," answered Mary. She added no more, and Carrie thought it was time to stop the questions.

"Belinda, are we putting sequins on this veil or is it to be plain?"

Belinda, taking her mother's hint, answered, "Just plain, Maw. That should save us some work. Sewing on sequins is a tedious job."

It was four o'clock when Carrie left the hotel, promising to return the next day. She hated being away from Nate, but she knew Belinda was desperate for the help. Ady Rose was to join them tomorrow, so there would be five of them sewing together.

On the way home she thought about Mary Carlisle and the story she had revealed to them. She could relate to Mary's feelings a little. There were times she'd almost hated Tom: not for herself, but for the way he treated his children. She had seen their hatred toward him grow, but the hate and bitterness she saw in Mary's eyes sent chills up her spine.

Please, Lord, take that hate away, her heart whispered.

"There's my Carrie," called Nate. He had walked all the way to the bottom of the hill to meet her. Taking her arm and planting a kiss on her lips, he asked, "How was my working woman's day? Do you know how much I missed you?"

"My day was good," she answered, "and, yes, I know how much you missed me, because that's how much I missed you. I have lots to tell you, though. We can talk while I fix supper."

"We can talk while we eat," said Nate, a mischievous look on his face. "I fixed supper."

Carrie stopped and looked up at him. "You did? You are the best husband in the world, Nate Swank!"

"Well, of course," he answered.

Nate had fried some ham, fixed mashed potatoes, and opened up a can of green beans. With it was some homemade bread Carrie had made the day before. It was a grand meal, and as they ate she told him about Mary and the terrible life she had lived as a child.

"That explains why she doesn't take to men too well," said Nate.

"We've just got to be her family now," said Carrie. "We can't make up for the past, but we can make her feel a part of our family and show her that not all men are like her stepfather. Can you imagine, seeing your own mother brutally killed?"

By the end of the week Carrie's work with Belinda was finished, and she could stay home with Nate. Sunday Sile J. came to church with Charles and Lucinda. He still had that sad, faraway look in his eyes, but at least he came. It was a beginning. Things settled down in the little neighborhood, and thankfully, there were no more fires.

On Tuesday of the following week, Carrie's telephone rang. She was used to it by then, and quietly answered. It was Amanda.

"Maw Carrie, I just wanted to let you know that Anja had her baby girl last night. I haven't seen it, but I talked with Trula and she said both mother and daughter are fine. The papa, however, is a wreck!"

Carrie laughed joyfully. "I am so happy for them, and for Homer and Trula. They deserve every chance to rejoice. I can't wait to see the baby. My, my! Lily is now a great-grandmother!"

"Trula says they will be staying with them for a few weeks, but then they will be moving to the new home they bought near the orphanage. I'd best get off the phone now. Just wanted you to know."

"Thank you, dear, for calling. Give my love to the kids."

"I will, Maw Carrie," replied Amanda. "Samuel is home sick today. I don't know if he's coming down with a cold, or maybe the flu. Say a little prayer for him."

With that they said their goodbyes, and Carrie whispered a prayer for her youngest grandson.

CHAPTER 12

In church on Sunday, Homer, every bit the proud grandpa, made the announcement to his congregation.

"Trula and I are proud and thankful to announce that our Matthew and our daughter-in-law Anja are the parents of a beautiful daughter. She has been named Kila Elaina after Anja's mother, who is Elaina Ilson, the dear woman who took care of our son when he was wounded. Anja and little Kila are both doing well."

The entire congregation applauded and shouted their praises to God. Then they were silent, as Homer seemed to have more to say.

"We have more joyful news. We have been saving our money, and with some help from those who wish to remain anonymous, we are able to have Anja's parents brought to America!"

This announcement brought gasps of surprise, and then thunderous applause and tears of joy.

"They will arrive in about three weeks, just as Matthew and Anja get moved into their new home. We thank all of you for your prayers, and we thank God for answering them. I know you will all make them welcome in our church and our little community. Now let's praise him in song. Turn to page ninety-four, 'Praise Him, Praise Him.'"

Homer was about halfway through his sermon when Carrie noticed one of the men go up and speak to Jessie. She had noticed Amanda and Samuel were not with him and the other two children today, but she had not had a chance to talk with him. Jessie leaned over and said something to Benjamin and Ivey, and then they all rose and left. An uneasy feeling tugged at her heart and she reached for Nate's hand. He squeezed her hand and nodded. After the service was over, she spoke to Luke and Syrena.

"Do you know if Samuel is all right?" she asked.

"I'm not sure," answered Syrena. "Yesterday he was still running a fever, and Amanda said he was just lifeless. She was thinking of calling Doctor White."

Just as she finished her sentence, they saw Benjamin running toward them.

"Maw Carrie, wait!" he called.

As he approached, Carrie could see the worry in his little-boy face. "What is it, Benjamin?" She asked, pulling him close.

"Papa says to tell you Samuel is terribly sick, and to come over if you can. Doc White is on the way."

"Maw," said Cindy, who had been waiting with them, "we'd better get the babies on home. Will you let us know how he is, and if we can do anything?"

Carrie reassured her, and she and the rest of the family headed toward Jessie's home. When they arrived, the others thought it best to wait on the front porch while Carrie and Nate went inside. Ivey was sitting in the living room, a frightened look on her young face. Nate nodded an unspoken message to Carrie, and went to sit with Ivey while she went on to the bedroom. Benjamin sat down with them and as Nate took the little girl in his arms, she burst into tears. As Carrie opened the bedroom door, she could hear Nate reassuring her.

The bedroom was shrouded in semi-darkness, and little Samuel looked small and frail as Carrie neared his bedside. Amanda rose from his bed and walked into her mother-in-law's arms. As Carrie held her, she could feel her shoulders shake and hear her gently sobbing. Jessie watched, feeling helpless.

"There, there," soothed Carrie. "I know you are worn out, Amanda, but our little Samuel is going to be all right. I've been praying for him."

For the first time, Carrie noticed Doc White's presence. He looked her way and she could see that his face was very solemn. Amanda left her and went back to sit by Samuel.

"Doc?" said Carrie, the question on her face. She and Jessie walked toward the doctor and he motioned toward the door. Once outside, he spoke in a low voice.

"I don't know what it is, Carrie. At least, I don't know for sure."

"What do you think it is?" asked Jessie. "Please, Doc, tell us."

Doc spoke reluctantly. "Well, he has a fever...a rather high one. He says his head hurts and his neck is stiff. He can hardly move it. I've seen these symptoms a few times before."

"So what is it?" asked Carrie. "No matter how bad, we need to know, Doc."

Hesitating again, Doc finally spoke. "It may be spinal meningitis."

Both Carrie and Jessie gasped.

"Now I'm not saying for sure that it is," said Doc. "I've just seen these symptoms before in patients who were ultimately diagnosed with spinal meningitis. It could be just a bad case of flu, but I believe it's more than that."

"How can you know for sure?" asked Jessie.

"He will have to have a spinal tap and blood work," Doc White replied. "I can't do that. I don't have the equipment or the facility."

"Then where?" asked Jessie.

"There's a place in Kentucky. I can set you up with a quick appointment. The trip will be hard on him, but I don't see any other way."

Jessie nodded. "Set it up, Doc. We'll get him there."

"Jessie," Doc continued. "I believe your brother lives near there. It's in Lexington. They also have housing there for families."

"I'm sure we could stay with Clay and his family," said Jessie.

Doc hesitated again. "I'm afraid that wouldn't be wise. You see, Jessie boy, if it is meningitis, it may be contagious. It all depends on the type. Some is and some isn't, but you don't want to take any chances."

"No," agreed Jessie. "I don't want to put Clay's family at risk."

"Okay," said Doc, picking up his bag. "I'm going to the office to make the appointment, and then I'll be back. Keep everyone away that doesn't need to be with Samuel. I'll leave it to the two of you to tell Amanda what we have talked about."

Jessie returned to the bedroom, and Carrie went to tell the others what Doc had said. She motioned for Nate to follow her to the front porch. Ivey had fallen asleep.

"Benjamin, would you stay with your sister a few minutes while Grandma Carrie and I go out and send the others home?"

"Sure, Grandpa," answered Benjamin, feeling proud that Nate had given him a job to do.

On the porch Luke, Ady Rose, Belinda and their families waited, along with Homer and Lily. Carrie told them what the doctor had said.

"What can we do?" asked Ady Rose.

"Just pray," replied Carrie. "Doc says no one should be around Samuel except those taking care of him. It may not be contagious, but we don't want to take chances. I'm going to stay the night and I would like Nate to stay, too, if you could milk and feed for us, Willy."

"Absolutely," said Willy, nodding. "We'll take care of things for as long as you need. We will also go by and tell Sile J. and the others what we found out."

As they were talking, Doc returned. "I made the appointment," he said. "They can see Samuel day after tomorrow, which means they will need to leave with him tomorrow. It will be a hard trip."

Carrie looked at the others and then asked in almost a whisper, "Doc, is there a chance Samuel could die from this?"

Doc looked at all of them. "I can't lie, folks. I have treated maybe six patients with spinal meningitis, and three of them have died. One other was left deaf. Two made a full recovery. The ones who died, however, were less than two years old. Samuel is older and stronger. Let's just pray that this little boy will be one of the lucky ones. But we may be getting ahead of ourselves. We don't know for sure yet that Samuel has meningitis. Like I said, it could just be a strain of flu. We can't know for sure until they do the tests."

"Will the tests tell us for sure?" asked Nate.

Doc nodded. "The spinal test will tell us. Until then, we can all spend some time on our knees. Now I would suggest that all of you go home and get some rest. There's nothing you can do here."

Doc went back into the house to tell Jessie and Amanda about the appointment and what he had worked out for them. After saying goodbye to the family, Carrie and Nate went back inside.

"Jessie, Amanda," said Carrie, after Doc White left, "you have a hard trip ahead of you tomorrow. If you will try to get some sleep, Nate and I will sit with Samuel. I promise we will take good care of him, and we'll call you if there's any change at all."

Jessie and Amanda looked at each other then nodded.

"Thanks, Maw," said Jessie. "I know you'll take good care of him, just like you did with all of us. I remember the time we thought Belinda was dying. You were by her side night and day."

Carrie placed her hand on his arm. "And just like Belinda healed, Samuel will also heal. We have to have faith."

Amanda nodded again. "If you and Papa Nate will get Benjamin and Ivey off to school tomorrow, I'm going to see if they can stay with Belinda and Joe while we're gone. Benjamin and Christopher are best friends, and Ivey adores Cammy. I think they would be satisfied staying there. School will be out for the summer in another week. Maybe Samuel will be better by then."

She wiped a tear from her eye. "I think I'll lie down for just awhile."

As they left the room, Carrie sat down in the chair beside Samuel's bed. Nate took a seat on the other side. "Such a sweet boy," said Carrie. "I know God has too many plans for him here to take him away." Then she began to hum.

A few hours later, there was a knock at the door. Jessie, who had laid down in the living room, rose to answer it. Belinda and Syrena stood on the porch, arms loaded with food.

"We knew Amanda wouldn't feel like cooking, but you need to eat," said Belinda. "We brought you some supper. She called me about keeping Ben and Ivey. Don't worry about them. We will love having them with us. Cammy is already planning some things to do with Ivey, and Christopher is excited about his best buddy coming over."

After they left, Carrie fixed the table with food while Nate and Jessie sat by Samuel. Amanda had heard the knock at the door, and came into the kitchen looking anxious and fatigued.

"You and Jessie eat while we sit with Samuel, and then we will eat," said Carrie.

Amanda looked at the food. "I'm not really hungry."

"I know you're not, dear," replied Carrie, "but you have some rough days ahead of you and you will need your strength. Try to eat for Samuel's sake."

Amanda simply nodded. Carrie left to summons Jessie.

Later, Amanda packed the things they would need while Jessie made arrangements for someone to fill in for him as sheriff while he was gone, and maybe even longer. Samuel was the most important thing right now.

"Did you find someone?" asked Nate, as Jessie returned to the bedroom.

"Yes, Beady Anders from over in Warren County is coming to take over for as long as he's needed, and Homer's son John is going to be helping him. John has been riding with me some, and he seems to have a real knack for the job. In fact, I've been thinking of asking the town council to make him my deputy."

Jessie and Amanda finally got to bed and Carrie sat across Samuel's bed from Nate, both watching him and praying. *Dear God,* prayed Carrie silently, *I'm here asking you for something again, but you said for us to ask, Lord, and to keep asking. I'm asking you to spare little Samuel and make him well. He's such a good little boy, and we all need him, especially his mommy and daddy. I just know you have big plans for him, and I'm going to put every ounce of my faith in you. You are a merciful God, and I thank you. Amen.*

As she finished her prayer, Samuel stirred and moaned, as though he felt her prayer.

"I'm here, Samuel," she whispered. "Grandma Carrie is right here."

"My head hurts, Grandma," he moaned, almost inaudibly.

Nate rose to go get a cool cloth for his head.

"I'll just rub your head," said Carrie softly. "I'll bet that will help, and Grandpa Nate will put a cool cloth on it."

As she rubbed the temples of his head, she sang a little song. "Jesus loves me this I know, for the Bible tells me so..." As she sang, Samuel drifted back into sleep.

They left for Kentucky early the next morning, and Carrie and Nate saw Benjamin and Ivey off to school. Neither wanted to go, feeling they were somehow letting Samuel down by going on with life as usual. Nate finally convinced them that Samuel would want to hear all about school when he returned home, and besides, after school they would be going to Belinda's. After they left, Carrie straightened the house while Nate went to see Luke. Then they headed for home, feeling extremely tired.

As they ate supper that night, Carrie and Nate talked about the events of the past days. She decided to go visit her brothers and Lucinda the following day. Carrie wanted to fill them in on what was happening, and check to see how they were doing in the homeplace.

It rained all night, and the pitter-patter of rain on the tin roof helped both Carrie and Nate get a restful sleep. The next morning, they arose early, finished their chores quickly, and headed out. As they walked out the door, Carrie inhaled the fresh moist air. The rain droplets on the leaves glistened like diamonds in the bright sunlight and she had to shade her eyes with her hand. It was a magnificent day. There was just something about a day after rain that made everything look cleansed and new.

"I'll go hitch up Fred and Ned," said Nate.

"Fred and Ned, my foot," returned Carrie, giving him a nudge.

"Bo and Peep?"

"Nate Swank, get out there and hitch those horses. I don't think you'll get a job in Hollywood as a comedian any time soon."

Nate pranced away, doing a little dance and singing, "Fred and Ned... Bo and Peep...I'll hitch you up and away we'll flee..."

"Doesn't rhyme!" she called after him.

Carrie shook her head and laughed. *He's trying to cheer me up, Lord. I do love that man.*

As they topped the hill and looked down on the homeplace, Carrie's heart filled as it always did. She was pleased as they neared the house to see how neat everything looked. It was lived in and loved once more. *Mama Cynth and Papa Silas would be pleased,* she thought with a smile of contentment. Just as they pulled in and brought the horses to a stop, Charles appeared from the old tool shed.

"Good morning!" he called. "That was quite a rain we had last night, wasn't it?"

"It looks like it was," answered Nate, "but we slept through it all. We sure needed the rain, though."

"Go on in, and I'll be in shortly," said Charles. "Lucinda and Sile are in the house."

Just then Lucinda appeared in the doorway. "Come on in! It's good to have company. I'm used to having the children and grandchildren around, and was feeling a little lonely."

As they went inside, they found Sile J. sitting in a rocking chair beside the window. Carrie gave Lucinda a questioning look and she simply shook her head. Carrie walked over and gave her brother a kiss.

"Well, Sile J., how does it feel to be back in our old home?"

For a moment he didn't answer. "It feels good and bad."

"How's that?" asked Nate.

"It brings back some good memories...but it brings back some bad ones, too."

"Tell you what," said Carrie, patting his arm. "Let's make some good new memories. We don't want to get rid of the good or bad from the past. They each have their place in our lives, but let's look toward the future and make lots of good ones. How about it?"

Sile didn't speak, but simply nodded, squeezing her hand.

"What's in the bag?" asked Lucinda, referring to the bag Carrie had hooked over her arm.

"Come look," said Carrie, sitting on the sofa.

Lucinda came to join her and Nate pulled a chair over to sit and talk with Sile J.

"I brought you some swatches of cloth," said Carrie, pulling them from the bag. "I thought you might want to start piecing a quilt or two. I also brought you two of Mama's quilt patterns. This one is the Little Dutch Girl, one of Mama's favorites."

"Oh, I love it," said Lucinda, taking it in her hand. "Thank you so much. I have a box of cloth swatches, too, and I'll pick out some for you when I can get around to it. We'll trade. What is the other pattern?"

"It's called a Fan Quilt, but it has pointed edges instead of round ones like most fans have. We always called it Mama's Pointy Fan Quilt."

"I like that," said Lucinda. "Oh, I can't wait to get started."

"How are things going?" asked Carrie quietly, changing the subject.

"Most things are going wonderfully well," replied Lucinda, "but not everything."

As she spoke, she gave a sideways nod toward Sile J.

Carrie looked sadly at her older brother and nodded.

Charles appeared in the doorway. "Nate, you and Sile J. walk outside to the tool shed with me. I want to show you my latest work."

Nate rose, and reluctantly, Sile J. joined him.

"Nothing seems to work," said Lucinda, after the men had left. "We try so hard to get him interested in the place, but it's like he's lost in a world he can't come back from. I just don't know what to do, Carrie."

"Just give it time," said Carrie. "Give it time, and we'll all pray. God will bring him back."

They talked on for a while, and Carrie told Lucinda about Samuel and all that was going on with him. They also talked about the homeplace and their plans for it.

"When are you going to start building a new barn?" asked Carrie.

"I don't think we will build it back," replied Lucinda. "Charles says we won't need it. We aren't going to raise hay, or keep cattle or horses. We just want a garden for food, and we can borrow horses to plow that or hire it done. We would like to keep one cow for milk and a few chickens. We're too old to try much beyond that."

"I can certainly understand that," nodded Carrie. "We're at the same place in our lives."

"Charles says we need to get a telephone," said Lucinda. "Do you think Luke might help us with that?"

"Oh, I'm sure he will," answered Carrie. "A telephone is a good idea in case of an emergency. I feel a lot more at ease since we got ours, especially with the fires we've had."

After another hour of visiting, Carrie and Nate took their leave, promising to keep Charles and the family up to date on the situation with Samuel. As they arrived home, Nate went on to unhitch the horses and Carrie went inside to fix some lunch. Just as she closed the door behind her, the telephone rang. It was Belinda.

"Maw," she said, "I tried earlier to get you. Are you okay?"

"Yes, dear. We went over to the homeplace to tell Charles and the family what is going on. Is something the matter?"

"Well, I don't really know. Jessie called earlier. He called here so he could check on the kids and deliver a message at the same time. They will be home day after tomorrow, and he said he will tell all of us then what they found out. I couldn't tell by his voice if the news was good or bad, but Maw, if it was good wouldn't he just go ahead and say so?"

Belinda didn't wait for her mother to respond. "Do you think you and Papa Nate could come to town so he can tell us what's going on? I called Ady Rose, Luke, and Cindy, and they'll be here."

"Yes, we will definitely be there," answered Carrie. "We all need to pray, Belinda."

As she hung up the phone, Carrie had a sense of foreboding. She couldn't explain it, and she hoped she was wrong, but she just had this ominous feeling crawling up and down her tired old spine. *Lord, I could sure use some reassurance right now,* she pleaded silently—but no reassurance came.

When Nate came in she told him about the phone call. He tried to hide his alarm, but she saw it in his eyes. "Whatever it is, Carrie love, He will give us the strength and faith to get through it."

CHAPTER 13

Carrie and Nate walked toward Haymaker, wanting to hurry, yet wanting to postpone what was to come. When they were in sight of Jessie's house, where they were to meet, Carrie stopped still in the street. Nate turned and took her arm.

"What is it, love?"

"Nothing. I'm all right," she said quickly. "Nate, just pray that I will act the way God wants me to act and say what He wants me to say. We have to be strong for Jessie."

"God will take care of us, Carrie," Nate reassured her. "Besides, we don't know if we're going to get good news or bad news."

"I just have this feeling..."

As they neared the front door of the house, they saw Ady Rose was just ahead of them and Cindy was coming up the street. Before they could even knock, Jessie opened the door.

"Come on in, everyone. Luke is already here."

His face showed no answers.

Amanda was just coming from Samuel's bedroom. She greeted them with hugs, and then they all sat down.

"I know you both must be absolutely worn out," said Carrie. "Did Samuel make the trip okay?"

Amanda nodded with a weak smile. "Actually he slept most of the time, and we were thankful for that."

"We won't delay this any longer," said Jessie. "I know you are all anxious to hear what the doctors in Kentucky had to say. First of all, Samuel does not have meningitis."

"Oh, praise God!" said Ady Rose, as everyone else gave a sigh.

"Doc White is not usually wrong," said Luke, "but I'm glad this time he was."

Carrie looked into Jessie's eyes...and then into Amanda's.

"There's more, isn't there, Jessie?"

He simply nodded his head, unable to speak. Amanda took a deep breath and spoke for him.

"The symptoms Samuel has are very much like the symptoms for meningitis. That is why Doc White misdiagnosed his illness."

"Then...what does he have?" asked Belinda, with hesitation.

Jessie looked at all of them with tears in his eyes.

"Samuel has polio."

There was complete silence in the room. No one was able to speak, yet the heavy silence screamed what they could not say. Finally, Luke found his voice.

"Polio?"

Again, complete silence.

Tears streamed from Jessie's eyes, saying what he could not.

"The early symptoms of meningitis and polio are much the same," said Amanda, almost inaudibly. "It is hard to tell which it is until fluid is drawn from the spine. The diagnosis is definite. Samuel has polio."

A chill enveloped the room as each one tried to accept what Amanda had said. Carrie felt herself tremble. There were no words to deal with the reality as their minds struggled to remember all they knew about polio. They looked from one to the other, not allowing their eyes to meet. If their eyes met there might be truth there, and they didn't want to see this awful truth.

"Maw?" said Jessie, a plea in his voice.

Carrie looked at her darling son and everything registered in her brain. She suddenly knew that right now Jessie and Amanda needed love, strength and reassurance. *Help me to help them,* God, she begged silently. And the strength came.

She walked to Jessie and put her arms around him, and as she did his composure collapsed. He did what his heart needed to do. He sobbed without restraint and, as he sobbed, Amanda's willpower gave way also. She moved to them and Carrie held them both. In seconds the entire family was holding each other, giving in to their fear and heartbreak. When their energy was spent, they simply sat there waiting...for what, they knew not.

Nate finally spoke. "I can't even imagine what you are going through right now. I can only tell you that we all love you, and we are here for you. Whatever you need, we will do. We will get through this as a family, and Samuel will get through this. You must believe that, because I believe it with all my heart."

"Thank you, Papa Nate," said Jessie. "We will need all of you during the next months, and yes, I do believe that Samuel will come through this and will be well. He's a strong little boy who loves life, and he will fight."

"What is the next step, Jessie?" asked Ady Rose. "What has the doctor told you?"

As Amanda slipped back to the bedroom to check on Samuel, Jessie told them everything the doctors had said and what they were facing in the coming months, and possibly years.

"First of all, Samuel seems to have a mild case, if there can be anything mild about polio. That's already one thing in our favor. Some die within a few days of being diagnosed. Some are paralyzed completely. Samuel's prognosis is much better than that. Right now only his legs are paralyzed. His breathing doesn't seem to be affected at all, which is the main thing that causes death in polio victims. Those who don't die are put in huge machines called iron lungs, which make them breathe. The doctors showed us pictures. They were hideous, and those people have to spend the rest of their lives like that. I couldn't bear that for Samuel, and yet we would do anything possible to keep him alive. He can swallow well also, although right now he has no appetite. There was stiffness in his neck, but that seems to be lessening. His fever is not as high. He is extremely tired and wants to sleep most of the time, but according to the doctor, right now that is a good thing because he needs his rest. The next few weeks will be crucial. He could still develop some of those problems."

"What kind of treatment does he require?" asked Belinda. "We'll all help with anything you need."

"Well," continued Jessie, seeming to search for words, "there is a place in Georgia called Warm Springs. Do you remember that President Franklin Roosevelt had polio?"

"Yes," answered Cindy. "We talked about it in school. He went down there for treatments and then...didn't he start some sort of treatment place?"

"That's right," nodded Jessie. "It involves something called hydrotherapy. Very warm water is supposed to help, so that the limbs don't become useless. The doctors are going to try to get him in there. He will have to stay a good while."

"Could you or Amanda stay with him?" asked Cindy. "He would be so scared by himself."

"Yes," Jessie replied. "We would both go down, and then Amanda could stay."

"Jessie, we love having Benjamin and Ivey with us," said Belinda. "You don't have to worry about them."

"Thanks, Sis. That means a lot."

"Son, I would be glad to go down and stay with him if Amanda needs to come home some," offered Carrie. "I know she will want to be with him, but she might need a rest now and then, too. Whatever you need, I am here. If you need money, anything we have is yours."

"The doctors say it won't cost us a thing," said Jessie, "except to get down there and back, and maybe a little for Amanda's meals. President Roosevelt also started a program called the March of Dimes, and it will pay for his treatments."

"Yes!" said Cindy, her eyes lighting up. "We read about that too, and remember the cards sent home for the children to put their dimes in?"

They all nodded.

"That is wonderful, Jessie," said Ady Rose. "See, God is already taking care of things."

"The thing is," said Jessie, continuing, "it will take awhile to get him in down there. In the meantime, we have to do warm water treatments here. We will have to put him in tubs of very warm water about five times a day. That's where we will need your help."

Everyone nodded.

"I need to go back to work—at least part time. We will need someone here with Amanda, to help her fill the tub and lift him in and out of it."

"I will help," said a voice from the doorway.

Everyone turned to see the source of the voice. There stood Sile J.

Amanda had just returned from the bedroom, and Sile J. walked over to her.

"I will help," he said again.

As Amanda's eyes met his, an understanding seemed to meld between them. She took his hand.

"Let me help,"

"Sile J., are you okay?" questioned Carrie, going toward him.

"Maw Carrie, he's okay," answered Amanda, holding up her hand.

Carrie seemed to sense that Amanda was trying to tell them all something, and she sat back down.

Sile J. continued to look at Amanda as he spoke. "It's been a long, long time since I've felt useful, and I need to feel that way again. I once had a little boy, and I loved him the way you love Samuel. I can help you, if you will trust me and give me a chance."

As Sile J. spoke, tears trickled unforbidden down his face.

Amanda looked at Sile. "I would be grateful for your help, Uncle Sile, and I have no doubt that you can give Samuel plenty of love. A mother knows these things."

She looked at the others. "Sile J. will be helping me every day with Samuel. I may need the rest of you to help some, too, but Sile J. will be my main help. You see, God sent him here today. I knew it the minute I looked into his eyes. We need him, and he needs to be needed."

Not a dry eye was to be found in the room, and no one doubted Amanda's words.

The plans were made. Luke or Jessie would go get Sile J. each morning. He would stay and help Amanda until Jessie got home in the afternoon. If needed, he would stay overnight. Each day, except on weekends, one of the others would come also to stay a few hours and give Amanda a break.

"Now, Uncle Sile," said Amanda, taking him by the hand, "I want you to come in and say hello to Samuel."

Sile J. followed her into the bedroom. They were there for about twenty minutes, and when they came back to the living room, Carrie could not believe the look on her brother's face. It glowed! She looked over at Nate, and it was obvious that he also saw the change.

Thank you, God, she whispered silently. *You've given Sile J. a reason to live again.*

Soon everyone took their leave. Tomorrow was Saturday, but Sile J. would be coming to begin his work and to meet Benjamin and Ivey. He headed toward home with a new bounce to his step and a look of joy on his face.

Sunday found all of them in church, including Sile J. He had obviously told Charles and Lucinda everything, and they were beaming.

"I can't wait to talk to you," Lucinda whispered to Carrie. "Will it be okay if I come over tomorrow?"

"Yes," answered Carrie. "We have much to talk about!"

On Monday, Sile J. arrived at his new "job" bright and early, delivered by Luke. Samuel's face lit up when he saw his "Uncle Sile."

Sile greeted him with a smile and a handshake. "Good morning, Samuel. You and I have a big day ahead of us. We're going to take warm baths for your legs and do exercises, and if you work really hard, I have some stories to tell you!"

"I'll work *very* hard, Uncle Sile," said Samuel. There was a touch of excitement in his weak voice.

As soon as Amanda had the water warm enough, Sile placed him in the tub. As he lay in the tub, Sile exercised his legs gently.

"Did you know I grew up here, Samuel?"

"Here in Haymaker?"

"Yes. My dad was a farmer, and he was a wonderful father, just like your dad. His name was Silas. I'm named for him—Silas Junior—but everyone always called me Sile J. Bet you didn't know that!"

"Wow!" said Samuel. "I've always just been called Samuel."

"Well, maybe when it's just you and me, I'll call you Samuel J. How's that?"

"Really, Uncle Sile? That would be super!"

"Then Samuel J. it is!"

By the time the warm bath was finished, Samuel was tired, so Sile J. dried him off, dressed him, and put him to bed. Then he went into the kitchen where Amanda was working.

"Our boy is down for a nap. What can I do to help?"

"Oh, Uncle Sile," said Amanda. "You are doing enough. Sit down and rest while you can."

"I don't see you resting," said Sile. "Now I need to feel useful. What can I do?"

"Well...I need some wood carried in so I can warm water for his next bath."

"Then you shall have it!" With that, Sile headed outside.

Bringing an armload in, he said, "I think we are going to need some more wood chopped. If you can keep an eye on the boy, I'll get busy with that."

By the time he had chopped more wood and carried another armload in, it was time for another bath for Samuel. Amanda heated the water and Sile J. filled the tub. Then he lifted Samuel into the tub.

"I'll exercise him this time," said Amanda. "You can rest."

"But, Mama," said Samuel, "Uncle Sile tells me stories."

Seeing the disappointment in Amanda's eyes, Sile J. knew she needed some time with her son.

"Let's let your mother do it this time, Samuel," he said. "I need to chop some more wood, and I need time to think about the story I want to tell you. Stories are better if you remember them just right."

Samuel smiled. "Okay, Uncle Sile. I'll bet it's gonna be a good one. Do you know any stories, Mama?"

"I surely do!" responded Amanda. "Did I ever tell you about falling in my daddy's fish pond?"

Sile J. laughed as he headed for the woodpile. It had been a long time since he had chopped wood. He couldn't remember it being so enjoyable.

Later that evening, as Carrie and Nate sat on the front porch, Luke came by. He told them all about Sile J.'s day with Samuel, as told to him by Amanda.

"I went by to see Samuel about three o'clock," said Luke. "You wouldn't believe the change in him. All he could talk about was Uncle Sile."

"God moves in mysterious ways," said Carrie. "This is nothing less than God using bad for good. Nobody wants Samuel to have polio, but God is bringing something good out of it. Mark my word, Luke, Samuel is going to be well and healthy again."

Luke rose to go, but just as he did, they heard a siren.

"A fire," gasped Carrie. "Oh, I had so prayed they were over. What could it be this time?"

"Let's ride into town and see," said Luke. "You two go with me, and I'll bring you home later. It's better than sitting here wondering."

Carrie and Nate agreed, but as they arrived in town, nothing could have prepared them for the sight.

"Oh, no!" cried Carrie. "The school! Oh, our precious school! Who would do such a thing?"

The flames were leaping high into the sky, hungrily devouring the little schoolhouse, feasting unashamedly on the books and papers and desks.

Nate joined Luke and all the others in trying to put out the fire, but it was too late. As the fire gave one horrible leap and bellow, the school was completely engulfed, collapsing in defeat. Carrie imagined that she could actually smell the books, chalkboards, and tools of education as they were lost forever. She stood, hand clasping her throat, too sad to even cry. As she looked around, almost everyone living in the little town was doing the same.

Thank God school was out for the summer, her heart spoke. *Thank God no child was hurt.* Then she thought of Landon, Cindy's husband. This wasn't just his job: it was his career, his love. Would he have a job now? Would there be money to rebuild the school? Almost as if he heard her thoughts, Landon appeared at her side.

"Oh, Landon, this is just terrible," she said, entwining her arm through his. "I'm so sorry this is happening."

"Me, too, Maw Carrie."

She could see the tears in his eyes.

He watched the burning building, seemingly unable to draw his eyes from the hideous taunting flames. "I feel pain for every book, every eraser, every desk..."

At his last words, a scream went up from the crowd.

"No! Someone help him! Oh, dear God, no!"

"What is it?" asked Carrie, stretching to see above the crowd. "What has happened, Landon?"

"It's Brady Coleman!" yelled someone in the crowd.

"What about Brady?" asked Carrie, of the person in front of her, but he simply shook his head.

"I'll be right back," said Landon, pushing his way through the crowd.

As Landon made his way to see what had happened, Carrie looked around the crowd at her friends and neighbors. Their expressions were a plethora of fear, sadness, anger, and confusion. To the left she spotted Mary Carlisle, standing alone watching the fire. Carrie couldn't read the expression on Mary's face.

She's been through so much sorrow and pain, thought Carrie. *I was hoping we could show her the goodness in people, but there is nothing good about this.*

Just as she started over to Mary, Landon returned, a grim look on his face made more ominous by the black soot smudges.

"It was Brady Coleman," he said. "He was trying to drag a desk out when a beam fell on him."

"Is he...?"

"Yes, Maw Carrie. I'm afraid he's dead."

"Oh, Landon," cried Carrie. "He has a wife, and three little boys! Why is this happening? Now it's more than just fire. Whoever did this has also killed someone."

She looked back over toward the place where Mary was standing, but she was no longer there.

It seemed that the fire continued forever, but by seven o'clock the flames had died out. All that was left were smoldering embers and a smell that tugged menacingly at each nose, a reminder of all that was lost. Nate, black from the fire, sweat making crooked paths down his face, came to find Carrie.

"We did all we could," he said, exhausted.

"I know you did," answered Carrie, soothingly, patting his tired face. "Everyone tried. It was just no use."

In a few minutes Luke came through the crowd, equally black and weary. "Let me take you two home. I know you are worn out."

As they rode home, no one could speak. The sight they had witnessed was just too heartbreaking to talk about. Luke let them out at the bottom of the hill with a promise to call or come by the next day. "Try to get some sleep," he said as he backed away.

Sleep was painfully elusive. Carrie kept seeing the flames, the smoke... remembering the smell. She kept imagining the sadness and pain of Brady Coleman's young wife. She kept seeing children with no school.

Nate awoke about three in the morning to find Carrie gone. Hearing a noise from the other bedroom, he pushed back the covers and went to look for her. Carrie was sitting at her sewing machine, her full attention on what she was sewing.

"Carrie, are you okay?" he asked.

Without looking around, she answered, "Yes, I'm okay. I just couldn't sleep. I'm sorry I woke you."

"What are you making?"

"I'm just making some little shorts for Samuel to wear when he has to take his warm water treatments. I thought it might make it a little more fun for him. See. These have frogs on them and the pair I've cut out over there have puppies on them. Do you think he will like them?"

Nate placed his hand on her shoulder. "He will love them, but you need to get some rest, Carrie. You will be completely exhausted."

"I just couldn't sleep," she said again. "I kept seeing the fire and the people, and thinking about Brady Coleman's wife and the sad children who have no father. My mind kept wondering what our children will do without a school. I had to do something to get it all out of my head. Nate, why is this happening? The other fires had to do with our family, but the schoolhouse involves everyone. Who could be so mean and uncaring? I don't understand it."

"Neither do I, love," he replied. "I think the person doing this is getting worse. I don't think it has anything to do with pranks. Whoever is doing this is filled with hate, and I just don't know anyone in Haymaker like that. Maybe it's someone who doesn't even live here."

"Can we go back into town tomorrow? Or I guess I should say today?" asked Carrie. "I want to find out more about it, and I want to go see Samuel. Maybe I'll have a pair or two of these shorts ready for him."

"Okay," answered Nate. "I guess there's no use in asking you to come back to bed. I'll just get dressed and make us some breakfast while you finish your sewing. Oatmeal okay?"

"That will be fine, Nate. Thank you. I'm not very hungry."

After breakfast, Nate went to milk the cow and do the feeding while Carrie finished the second pair of shorts for Samuel. At about ten o'clock they headed for town. Before they were halfway, they could smell the smoke and it brought back the scenes from yesterday. Tears sprang to Carrie's eyes. Her heart cried out to the Lord: *Lord help me to be strong today. It won't help anyone if I act weak.*

In answer to her prayer, Carrie felt strength creep into her body. She would be strong and wise in her behavior and her words. The entire community was hurting, and she would not add to that hurt. She would offer words of love and encouragement, and her first opportunity came almost immediately.

As they neared the school, she saw Jessie working in the rubble, writing something in a little notebook. When he looked up, she saw the pain and fatigue in his face. It was enough that he was facing the illness of his little son, but now this added to his heavy load. Beady Anders was stooped down a few feet from him, searching through the ashes. Just a few feet from Beady, Homer's son John was doing the same.

Jessie called to them. "Hi Maw, Papa Nate! I figured you two might be in town today. Looks like we have us a real mess here, doesn't it?"

Carrie kissed his cheek. "Yes, son, it does, but you are good at clearing up messes, and I have no doubt you will get to the bottom of all this."

"Let's just hope it's soon," he replied. "We're having a town council meeting this evening, and they are going to want some answers. Right now, I have none...except I know the fire was set intentionally, just like the others. I've got to find out who is doing this, Maw. Would you pray for God to lead me in the right direction? I don't want any more fires, and I surely don't want anyone else getting hurt or killed."

"I will most assuredly pray, Jessie. I know you will find this person."

"Jessie, have you given any thought to the idea that this person might be mentally sick?" asked Nate.

Jessie nodded. "Yes, I have. I'm almost sure it's not a prankster. I think the person is either mentally ill or has some sort of vendetta. The trouble is, no one in the community fits that description. We have people who don't like each other, but no one filled with this kind of vengeance or hate, and I don't know of anyone this mentally deranged."

"I don't either, Son," said Nate, shaking his head. "Have you thought about setting up watch teams to keep an eye on everything and report anything suspicious?"

"Beady and I were just talking about that earlier," replied Jessie. "I think I may bring that before the town council. I think we could get enough volunteers, after what happened here, to set up teams throughout the day and night."

After talking a little longer, they left Jessie to his work and headed toward his home to see Samuel. Amanda answered the door, looking almost as tired as Jessie.

"Oh, Amanda," said Carrie, hugging her daughter-in-law, "you look so tired. Is Samuel worse?"

"No, Maw Carrie," she answered. "It's just this, plus the fire, plus waiting for a call from Georgia and wondering if they can help Samuel. I'm just at my wit's end."

"Is Sile J. here?"

"Yes, he's in with Samuel. We just finished a warm water bath, and he's drifting off to sleep. I don't know what I would do without Uncle Sile. He was truly sent to us by God."

"Tell you what," said Nate. "Carrie and I want to see Samuel. Why don't we stay here awhile, and you get out and get some fresh air? Sile J. will be here, too, so he will be well taken care of."

"I could use some time outside," agreed Amanda. "I think I'll just take you up on that. Let me go fix up a bit. I might go by and say hello to Jessie."

She was ready to go in a matter of minutes, and after she left, Carrie and Nate went into the kitchen. The breakfast dishes had not been washed so they took to the task, feeling good that they could do something to help. Before they were halfway through, Sile J. joined them.

"Well," he said, "have you two hired on as kitchen help?"

"That we have," laughed Nate. "Is our boy asleep?"

Sile J. nodded. "Yes, he will probably sleep for a couple of hours. The water treatments wear him out."

"I'm so glad you can help them, Sile," said Carrie. "They really need you."

"Oh, it's the other way around," said Sile. "I'm the one who is getting the most out of this. That little boy sleeping in there has given me a reason to live again."

Carrie smile, then paled, as if an awful thought had crossed her mind. "Sile, what will you do when they take him to the hydrotherapy place in Georgia?"

"I'll wait for him to get back," answered Sile, emphatically. "And while I'm waiting, there are other children who need me. There's little Ivey. She's really sad and confused because of her little brother's illness. She needs someone to be there for her and love her and tell her stories. Benjamin tries to be brave, but he's scared, too. Oh, I have found there are lots of boys and girls who need just a little extra love and attention, and most of them love to hear stories."

Carrie gave her brother a hug. "I am so proud of you, Sile, and you know what? Lula would be proud of you, too."

"She wouldn't be proud of the way I've acted since she passed on," said Sile J. "Lula loved life and she loved people. I reckon she would take a stick to me for the way I've been acting. Now, while you two clean the kitchen, I'm going to chop some more wood and carry it in. We'll have more water to heat soon."

Carrie did every bit of work she could find to do, and when that was done she set to making some of her yeast bread and a couple of chocolate pies. She was sure Amanda didn't have time for much cooking. It was a good three hours before Amanda returned, looking just a bit more rested.

"Oh, Maw Carrie!" she exclaimed. "Thank you for all that you've done. After I went by to see Jessie I went by the mercantile. Luke was there and he insisted upon watching the store while Syrena and I went to the diner for some lunch. I don't know when I've relaxed that much."

"It's good for you, dear. The more relaxed you are, the better you can handle all that you are going through. Now I have some more water on heating and Nate and Sile J. are in with Samuel. I brought him a gift, so I'll just take it in to him before we have to leave. I want to go by the dress shop as we head home."

Carrie took the little shorts in to Samuel. His eyes showed his appreciation.

"I like them, Grandma Carrie. It'll be almost like going for a swim."

Sile J.'s eyes twinkled. "Now that just reminds me of a time I went swimming with my brothers. Yep, I'll have a swimming story to tell you while we do your exercises!"

With lighter hearts, Carrie and Nate left for the dress shop and a visit with Belinda. As they started down the street, Nate stopped. "Carrie, why don't I go visit a spell with Luke while you have some woman-time with Belinda?"

Carrie agreed and they went their separate ways, planning to meet at the dress shop in about an hour. As she opened the door to the dress shop, the little bell tinkled.

"Come in!" called a woman's voice. Carrie knew immediately that it was Mary Carlisle.

"Hello, Mary," she said, giving the young woman a warm hug. "What are you working on today?"

"Come look," said Mary, taking Carrie by the arm.

Carrie was still amazed at the change in Mary from the quiet, withdrawn woman who first came to Haymaker, to the warm outgoing woman she now saw.

"We are working on another bridal gown," she said. "This is for someone all the way over in Warren County. We are to make the bridal gown and six bridesmaids' dresses, and we only have a month to get it done!"

"My," said Carrie. "The dress shop is certainly making a name for itself."

"Yes, it is," laughed Belinda, coming into the room. "I never imagined we would have all the business we now have. This bride is a cousin to the one we just sewed for, so she was pleased enough to recommend us."

Just then Nettie came in carrying two bolts of cloth in a beautiful azure blue.

"This just arrived. Ain't it the prettiest color? I can't wait to see the dresses we make from it. Oh, hi, Miss Carrie."

"Hi, to you," laughed Carrie. "Looks like you girls are busy. If I stay long, you'll put me to work."

"Well...actually..." said Belinda. "We may need your help in a few days. Besides this wedding, we have four more dresses and several shirts to get made. Think you might give us some of your time, Maw?"

"I'm sure I can," Carrie answered. "I could also do some sewing at home."

"Have you been over to the schoolhouse?" asked Nettie. "Ain't it just awful?"

Carrie nodded. "Yes, it is. It breaks my heart...and do you know what breaks my heart even more?

The others waited.

"It breaks my heart that anyone could do something like this. I really hurt for that person."

"One thing I've learned," said Mary. "You just never can tell about people. They can put on a front, but they may be an entirely different person inside."

"Ain't that the truth!" said Nettie, pursing her lips in anger.

Carrie soon took her leave to meet Nate and head home. They walked leisurely, arm in arm, feeling much lighter of spirit than when they came to town earlier.

"It's so good to see Sile J. alive and active again," said Carrie. "I know Charles and Lucinda must be extra happy. Have you ever stopped to think, Nate, that they gave up their life in Ohio and left their children behind to make a happier life for Sile J.? Now, that's love."

CHAPTER 14

The sultry sun of summer beamed down on the town of Haymaker and the surrounding community. Life went on as it has a way of doing, weaving its web of ups and downs, happiness and sadness, tears and laughter. The town council had agreed to set up watch teams to help prevent more fires, and there were enough volunteers for six teams, with a four-hour watch for each. They would keep their eyes open to report anything suspicious. Beyond that, no one had an idea or solution. Luckily, they gave Jessie a vote of confidence and asked Beady Anders to stay on for a while to help. They also agreed to give consideration to making John a deputy. Exactly three weeks after Jessie and Amanda returned home from Kentucky with Samuel, the call came from Georgia. Samuel was to be down there June the fifteenth, less than a week away. The family was both relieved and apprehensive: excited to finally get treatment for him, but anxious to see if it would help make Samuel well again.

Samuel's main concern was leaving Uncle Sile.

"But Uncle Sile can do my treatments," he said, puckered face proclaiming his unhappiness. "I don't want to leave Uncle Sile!"

"But, Samuel," persuaded his mother, "you want to be well again. Soon you can run and play with Benjamin and Ivey. Don't you want that?"

Samuel's mouth puckered again. "Yes, but Uncle Sile can help me get well."

At this Sile J. spoke. "Now, Samuel J., I don't like to hear you talk like this."

Samuel's eyes grew wide. Sile J. had never scolded him before.

"Samuel, you have to go down there and get well. You need to walk again, 'cause you and I have things to do. I'll be right here waiting when you return. Besides, I need time to think of more stories to tell. You've just about worn out my story box."

"Your story box?" said Samuel, confusion wrinkling around his eyes.

"Absolutely!" exclaimed Sile J. "That's the little box in my heart where I store all my stories. Sometimes it gets empty, and I have to give it time to fill up again. Tell you what…I have just a few left. I'm going to write them down on paper. I'll give them to your mother, and once a week—*if* you work really hard—she will pull out one of those stories and read it to you."

"You will, Uncle Sile? You'll write them down? Then it will be like you're there with me!"

"That's exactly right," avowed Sile. "Don't you ever doubt, my Samuel J, old Uncle Sile will be there with you every single day, right here in my heart—'cause Uncle Sile loves you!"

As Sile J. pointed to his heart, tears came to his eyes, but not only to his. Amanda and Jessie were fighting tears, also.

Sile, true to his word, showed up to say goodbye to his "best buddy" on their day of departure, stories in hand. He gave them to Amanda.

"Now Mrs. Amanda," he said, loud enough for Samuel to hear, "You read one of these to Samuel J. each week, *if* he works really hard. You'll know just when to read them."

With this he turned to Benjamin and Ivey. "Now, you two need to be ready early tomorrow morning, 'cause we're a'going fishing. See if your pal Christopher wants to go with us, and tell Mrs. Belinda to be ready to fry fish for supper."

At this, two sad, forlorn faces lit up. The two clapped their hands. "We'll be ready, Uncle Sile!"

Sunday morning as Carrie and Nate arrived at the church yard, they spotted Sile J. surrounded by children. Charles and Lucinda were watching from the church steps.

"What's going on?" Carrie asked.

Charles laughed. "Well, it seems our brother knows how to win the hearts of all the children in Haymaker. He brought sticks of gum for each one!"

"Oh, that's wonderful," laughed Carrie, clapping her hands.

"Yes, it is," agreed Lucinda. "I am so happy to see Sile J. alive again. I can't wait to write to Orin Tate to tell him."

As church began, Pastor Homer had a special prayer for Samuel. Carrie glanced across the aisle at Benjamin and Ivey. Benjamin, though sad, seemed to be handling the situation well, perhaps because he was with his best buddy, Christopher. Ivey, on the other hand, looked ready to burst into tears at any moment. Belinda, aware of Ivey's sadness, bent to say something to her. Carrie saw the little girl nod as her face lit up. She rose from her pew and went to sit with Sile J. Showing no surprise at all, Sile J. put his arm around the little girl and she lay her head over on his chest, as if to absorb comfort from him. Sile J. looked across the aisle at Belinda and nodded.

Then Pastor Homer had an announcement to make.

"I'm very happy to tell you that this coming Friday, Anja's parents, Mr. and Mrs. Eli Ilson, will finally be arriving. I know you will all make them welcome. It is not easy for them to leave their homeland and the only home they have ever known to come all the way to America. Please help us make them glad they have come. Next Sunday, after church, we will be having a small reception for them at Matthew's and Anja's home. Their house is small, so we will use the front porch and yard, as well. If the weather is not good, Sarah McLindy has graciously offered the dining room of the boarding house."

As they rode home in Willy's car, Carrie and Ady Rose talked about the upcoming event.

"We should offer to help with refreshments. Don't you think so, Maw?" said Ady Rose.

"Definitely. I'll call Trula tomorrow and see what we can bring."

All the children came to Carrie's for lunch except Jessie and Amanda. Belinda brought Benjamin and Ivey with her family. Cindy and Landon arrived with the twins, who were growing like morning glory vines. Daniel was even cutting his first tooth. After their meal, talk turned to the school-house fire.

"Will they build a new school before time for the kids to start back?" asked Cammy, looking to Landon for an answer.

"I hope so, Cammy," he answered. "We have sent a request to Richmond, asking the state to provide finances for it. We even have volunteers to do the construction, if the state will give the money. I just hope we'll hear soon, and the construction can begin. It will take every bit of the summer to get it built."

"What if they don't give the money?" asked Ethan, who had been listening closely.

"Well, then we will have to find a place to meet for classes," Landon responded, tapping Ethan on the shoulder. "Different classes could meet in different places, if necessary."

"What do you mean?" Ethan asked.

"The church would be available. Maybe a couple of grades could meet there. Then a grade might meet at the orphanage. Possibly my mother would let a grade meet in her dining room at the boarding house, since she only serves breakfast and supper. We will find a way, Ethan."

Talk then returned to the fires. "Are they any closer to finding the culprit?" asked Willy.

Luke shook his head. "Not really, but you know I'm sure we will soon, since we have volunteers watching things closely. Even today we have a crew watching the town and surrounding area."

"Do you think that will really help?" asked Mary Carlisle, who had joined the family for lunch. "I mean, this person is evidently pretty sly, and he probably knows about the watch teams."

Luke nodded. "You're right, Mary, but if this person is deranged, he won't be able to keep from starting the fires. If he is just plain mean, he will think he can outsmart the teams. If he's not from Haymaker, he may not know about the watchers."

"I just hope they find this person soon," said Ady Rose, "before half the area goes up in flames."

"We all hope that," agreed Mary.

"Let's change the subject," injected Syrena. "This fire talk depresses me. Maw Carrie, do you know how long Jessie, Amanda, and Samuel will be gone?"

"Not for sure," answered Carrie. "At least four weeks for Amanda and Samuel. Jessie should be back in a few days."

"I pray the treatments will help," said Syrena. "Samuel is such a sweet little boy, and so full of life. I want to see him run and play again. By the way, why didn't Sile J., Charles, and Lucinda come for lunch?"

"They were having lunch with Homer and Trula," answered Carrie. "Homer wanted to talk to Sile J. about something. I have no idea what it was."

Nate took Carrie's hand. "We're just happy to see Sile J. full of life again. The children all love him, that's for sure."

Talk continued among the adults while the children played their games of tag, Mother May I, Simon Says, and various other games country children loved to play. As the afternoon wore on, they began to take their leave, and before long Carrie and Nate were alone again.

Jessie came home two days later and after going by to see his children, he came to see Carrie and Nate. Carrie could read her son's expression, and knew he was harboring fear and desperation.

"Tell us everything, son," said Nate. "What did you find out in Warm Springs?"

"There's really not much to tell," answered Jessie. "They will be doing hydrotherapy treatments every day for the next four weeks. Only then will they know if the treatments help. It is most likely they will have to fit him with leg braces and the metal crutches, and he will have to go back for more treatments. They say four weeks of treatments is usually not enough."

"Will he be able to walk with the braces and crutches?" asked Carrie.

Jessie shook his head. "We don't know. Everything now is about waiting...and it's all so uncertain." A tear slid down his face.

Give me the right words, Lord, Carrie pleaded silently as she reached for Jessie's hand.

"Maw, do you think all of this is happening because of what I did to Pa? Do you think God is punishing Samuel because of me?"

Carrie took a deep breath. "Son, there are not a lot of things I know for certain, but this is one I do know. I can tell you without a single doubt, that is not God's way. This has nothing to do with you and your paw. You were just a boy when all that happened, Jessie. No, God doesn't work that way."

"Are you sure, Maw?"

"Without a doubt, Son. Now you put that out of your mind. You need God's healing hand on Samuel now, so don't be thinking of blame. Just think of His mercy and love, and tell him you need a heaping dose of it. As much as you love that little boy, God loves him more."

Jessie took Carrie's hand in his and kissed it. "What would I ever do without you, Maw?"

He left soon after that, a little lighter of heart, anxious to take Benjamin and Ivey back home with him. Tomorrow he would go back to work.

On Friday, Amanda called Jessie to report that the treatments were going well, but both she and Samuel were homesick.

"He tries to be brave during the day," she told Jessie, "but he cries every night when he goes to bed. He misses you, and Benjamin and Ivey, and Uncle Sile J. He makes everyone down here call him 'Samuel J.,' and if they don't, he won't answer them. Our little boy can be quite stubborn sometimes."

Jessie laughed. "That's okay. I'm glad he's feeling well enough to show some spunk."

On Sunday, Carrie and Nate parted at the church. She went on to help with the reception for Mr. and Mrs. Ilson. As she neared Matthew's and Anja's little house, she could see people already at work. Floyd and John were carrying tables from the boarding house, with Sarah McLindy following along, giving orders. Matthew and Mark were following along with extra chairs. Apparently Mark had obtained permission to come home from school for the family event.

"Hi, Miss Carrie!"

She saw Mary Carlisle waving to her.

"Bring your food over here. We have this table ready."

"You're an early bird today, Mary. It's good to see you."

"Oh, you have no idea how early," said Mary, stifling a yawn. "I've been up since four this morning."

"My! What got you up that early? You're not sick, are you?"

"Oh no," answered Mary, with a shake of her head. "I joined the fire watch team on Sunday mornings from four to eight. It's the only time I'm free to do it, and I wanted to do my part."

Carrie gave Mary a hug. "That is good of you, dear. You are becoming a part of our little community."

Just then Beady Anders walked their way. Carrie was surprised to see Mary blush.

"Good morning, Mrs. Swank," he said, nodding to Carrie. "And how are you, Mary?"

Mary blushed again. "I'm fine, Beady. A little sleepy maybe."

"Yeah, four o'clock was a little early, wasn't it?" said Beady. "At least we had a quiet watch. Are you going to be on the team every Sunday?"

Mary nodded. "Those are my plans. I wish I could do more, but with my work at the orphanage and dress shop, plus the work I take home, there's just no more time."

"You can only do what you can do," said Beady, straightening his shoulders as if he had coined the statement all by himself.

Carrie watched the exchange with amusement. *Well, Lord, it looks like our Mary is becoming a part of the community in more ways than I thought.*

As Beady went on his way, Carrie smothered a giggle. Mary looked over at her.

"Now, Miss Carrie, don't go making something out of nothing, you hear!"

At the look on Mary's face, Carrie broke out in laughter. Luckily, they were interrupted.

"My, the Lord has blessed us with a magnificent day for this reception," said Sarah McLindy. "I hope we have plenty of food. I hear most of the folks from the Primitive Baptist church will be coming by to give their regards to the Ilsons."

Mary, thankful for Sarah's interruption, made a quick getaway to help with the other tables being set up. Carrie could hardly contain another fit of laughter. As other women brought their food, though, her mind had to return to the mission at hand. It did, indeed, look to be a perfect day for a community get-together.

Just as everything was set up and ready, church let out and people began coming from all over the town and little Appalachian community.

Women were still bringing food, and the biggest problem had become finding a place for it all. Homer and Trula came with the Ilsons between them.

"May I have everyone's attention?" Homer shouted over the joyful noise of celebration. "I want to introduce our honored guests to all of you."

Some of the men had made a platform for the occasion, and he led the Ilsons up on it.

"I would like you to make welcome in our town and in our hearts, Eli and Elaina Ilson."

A roar of applause went up from the crowd.

"As you know, Eli and Elaina are the parents of Anja, our dear daughter-in-law. They are also the ones who took care of our Matthew, and nursed him back to health when he could have died. They also hid him from the Germans. We owe them more than we could ever repay."

There was another roar of applause.

"I would like to ask Eli to speak a word or two."

Eli Ilson walked to the front of the platform. He was a slight figure of a man, but he held himself erect with a humble dignity that bespoke kindness, yet demanded respect. He reached for Elaina's hand, pulling her to his side.

He spoke in stilted English. "Elaina and I are most glad to come to be in your little town. We have missed our daughter Anja much, and now we have a beautiful granddaughter. God has blessed us. We were glad to have Matthew in our home. War is a terrible thing, but sometimes it can bring good people into our lives. That is what it did for us."

The crowd once more broke into applause.

Eli continued. "In Tournai we owned a little farm to provide what little food we had. At one time, I even had a little clock shop. I hope to find work here. I am old, but not too old to work. I want to earn my way. It is good to be here. Thank you."

After more applause, Homer spoke again. "We will now say our thanks to God and the Ilsons will lead us in line to do what we do best—EAT!"

Carrie, standing beside Nate, watched as everyone took their place in line. No one minded the wait. It gave them more time to talk and catch up on all the news. Just then, someone tapped Carrie on the shoulder. She turned and gasped to see Homer's Luke, smiling from ear to ear.

"Why Luke!" she exclaimed, giving him a crushing hug. "It is so good to see you. How are things going on the horse ranch? Is my son treating you well?"

Before he could answer, Cindy walked up. "He'd better treat you well," she said, "or his baby sister will be onto him."

"Oh, he is treating me very well," he answered. "I have never been happier."

Suddenly Luke blushed. Turning around, he/ pulled a lovely, young red-haired woman to his side.

"I have met someone who has added to my happiness. I would like you to meet Jenny MacGregor. Jenny is a schoolteacher in Lexington, and we met at a church social."

"It's nice to meet you, Jenny. I'm Carrie Swank and this is my husband Nate."

"And I am his cousin, Cindy. I am also a schoolteacher—or I was, until our twins were born. Now I'm very much a mother. That's my husband over there with our sons. His name is Landon McLindy."

Jenny smiled, and then her smiled turned to a look of confusion.

Cindy began to laugh. "I know exactly what's going through your mind, Jenny. I get the same expression from everyone. Yes, my name is Cindy McLindy! That is my cross to bear for falling in love with that handsome guy over there."

"Oh, I didn't mean to..." Jenny stopped, at a loss for words.

"I will get my revenge, though," continued Cindy, a mischievous look on her face. "When we have a daughter I will name her Mindy McLindy, or maybe Wendy McLindy."

Jenny looked at her, disbelief enveloping her face. Then she saw the twinkle in Cindy's eye and they both broke into laughter.

Cindy took her by the arm. "Come on, my new friend. I want you to meet my boys."

The two new friends walked away, leaving Luke to stare after them.

"Son, you might as well go with them," laughed Nate. "Those two look like trouble to me, and they'll need someone to bail them out eventually."

"Nate, you go on and get your food," said Carrie. "It looks like Lily and Mary could use some help over at the dessert table. I'll get up with you later."

"Just don't get in trouble with Cindy and Jenny," teased Nate, walking away.

As she arrived at the dessert table, Lily handed her a knife. "Here, Sister, slice some of those cakes. These folks are eating faster than I can slice."

It kept them busy for the next half hour, just keeping pies and cakes sliced and ready to dole out. It was pleasant, though, as she was able to talk to her sister and Mary as they worked. Eventually, Mary asked to take some time away and Carrie saw her walking toward Beady, who was waiting for her.

"I believe our Mary may have a beau," said Carrie.

"Well, at least some of the men around here have good eyes," said Lily. "Mary is a beautiful woman."

Floyd came to the dessert table just then.

"What's good over here, ladies?" he asked.

"Floyd, it all looks good to me," responded Carrie. "I'm so tired of slicing, though, I may not want to look at cakes, pies, and cobblers for a while. I think people should stick to making cookies."

At his request, Lily dished him up two kinds of cake and some peach cobbler. There was a chair nearby, so he sat down there to eat. Carrie and Lily pulled up chairs to take a break.

"Looks like might nigh everybody showed up today," said Floyd.

"We do have a good crowd," acknowledged Carrie.

"I think everybody smelled the food," said Lily. "Never saw so much eating going on in all my born days. I believe I'll go get me one of Ida Hanson's ham biscuits before they are all taken."

She walked toward the meats, leaving Carrie and Floyd.

"How are things going at the orphanage?" Carrie asked, making conversation.

"Keeping us busy, keeping us busy," said Floyd, as if saying it twice emphasized the situation. "These fires around here are keeping everybody busy, too, it seems."

"Oh, those fire sirens just send cold chills up my spine," said Carrie. "I just wonder where the fire is this time. I hope these watch teams will put a stop to them."

Floyd shook his head. "I doubt if that will happen. This person has a bone to pick, and he ain't gonna stop until he's picked it clean or until they catch him."

"Do you really think he will keep setting the fires, Floyd?" asked Carrie, a look of despair settling on her face.

"Yep! I do believe that," answered Floyd. "In fact, I can almost guarantee it."

With this he fell silent. Carrie looked at him, a feeling she couldn't explain threading its way along her spine.

"Got my ham biscuit," called Lily, returning to her chair. "In fact, I got me two of them. You wouldn't believe how food is going. I don't believe these people have eaten for a week."

Before Carrie and Nate left, they went over to speak to Eli and Elaina Ilson. When they found them, Luke and Syrena were talking to them and Eli's face was glowing.

"Yes," he was saying. "Yes, I would like that very much. You will not be sorry. I am a good worker."

"Hi, Maw, Papa Nate," said Luke. "Syrena and I have some new help in the mercantile. Eli has agreed to come work for us."

Eli stood next to Luke, his face still beaming. "It will be a good job for me. I do not like to just do nothing. I can make a life here for Elaina and me. Is good."

The mercantile had been back in business a few weeks now, and was keeping Luke and Syrena busy.

Carrie nodded. "That's wonderful, Luke. It will be good for all of you. You will have more time with each other and the children."

"I don't know about the children," laughed Syrena. "I think all the children are mesmerized by Sile J. He's all they talk about. He reminds me of the story about the Pied Piper. Wherever Uncle Sile goes, the children follow."

After a few more words, Carrie, Nate, Luke, and Syrena walked away. Syrena entwined her arm through Carrie's. "Maw Carrie, there's another reason Luke and I need help at the mercantile. We wanted to make sure before we told anyone, and you are the first to know."

Carrie looked at her daughter-in-law. The glow was there. How had she missed it?

"Are you...?"

"Yes, we are going to have a baby!"

"Oh, that is wonderful news," cried Carrie, hugging first Syrena, then Luke.

"We didn't think we were going to have anymore," said Luke. "We thought Mary Alice and Jacob would be all for us, but God is giving us a bonus. God is good, Maw!"

"Yes, He is, my darling son," agreed Carrie, a mixture of tears and laughter. "Yes, He is."

Carrie and Nate walked home, arm in arm, thinking about the day, smelling the honey suckle, and counting their blessings.

"What a glorious day," whispered Carrie.

CHAPTER 15

Samuel continued with his treatments in Warm Springs, and Amanda called once or twice a week to give a report. In one more week, he would get to come home for a month, but would then go back for four more weeks of treatment. He was walking a few steps now with braces and crutches, so there was improvement. This helped them all to deal with the time apart and the disruption of their happy little family.

Sile J. was still the hero of all the children, and they soon found out what Homer wanted to talk to him about. Sile and Charles came to see Nate one day.

"Homer wants me to start a baseball team," said Sile J.

"A baseball team?" said Nate, completely taken by surprise.

"Yep! That's what he had on his mind. I told him I'd let him know. If we do it, I'll need some help getting everything planned out. I'll need equipment, umpires, planners, and even uniforms."

"Goodness," gasped Carrie. "You have a lot going on in that head of yours, Sile."

"Well, I'd like to do it, Sis. I think it would be a good thing for the children, and the rest of the town. With all the tension and upheaval brought on by these fires, our little community could stand some pepping

119

up. I can't do it without help, though. Charles says he'll help. Lucinda even offered to help, if there is anything she can do."

Carrie saw the excitement in his face. "Then I think you should do it. Count Nate and me in."

"Good," said Sile, smiling like a little boy. "Good. Nate, will you be an umpire?"

Nate looked surprised. "Well, I don't know how good I'll be, Sile, but I'll do my best. I'm willing to learn."

Then Sile J. looked at Carrie. "Sis, I know this will be a lot of work, but do you think you and some of the ladies could make uniform shirts for the kids? I think shirts will be all they'll need. How about it?"

"I'm sure we could do it," replied Carrie. "I'll talk to Belinda, and I'm sure some of the other mothers could help out. Lucinda can help, too."

"Thanks," said Sile. "Thank you both. I just wish my little buddy Samuel could take part."

Carrie saw his look of excitement suddenly turn to sadness.

"Sile J., he may not be able to play right now, but who knows about a few months from now? He may be hitting homeruns in every game."

Sile J. smiled. "We just have to keep the faith, don't we?"

"You got that right," said Nate.

The fun and laughter of the Ilson reception was forgotten in one shrill moment.

The fire siren sounded loudly, instilling fear and disappointment in the hearts of those within its range. What could it be this time?

It was the middle of the night, and Carrie and Nate awakened instantly. Neither said a word, but they held each other tightly. After the initial fear faded, Nate spoke.

"Maybe they caught the fire in time."

"We can only pray," said Carrie, still holding on to Nate as if he could make it all go away. "I wonder what it is."

Sometime before dawn, they both drifted off to sleep once more. They were awakened by the ringing of the phone. At first, still half asleep, Carrie thought it was the fire siren again. Realizing it was the phone, she pushed back the covers and padded to the living room.

"Hello!"

"Maw, it's Luke."

"Oh, Luke, I'm so glad you called. Is it about the fire?"

"Yes. I knew you would be worried and wondering. Everything is okay, Maw. The fire was in the church, but it was seen by the watch team almost immediately. It did a little damage to the back entrance, but that's all. It can be fixed in no time. The smell is the worst of it, but a little airing out will take care of that."

"Thank God!" exclaimed Carrie, relief spreading quickly through her body. "But...the church? Why would anyone want to burn down the church?"

"I don't know, Maw," Luke replied. "Why do they want to burn down any of the buildings? I'm convinced the person is mentally unbalanced."

After a few more words, Luke said goodbye. He was going to the church to help with anything he could. Mr. Ilson had already begun his job at the mercantile. Carrie went back and sat on the bed next to Nate.

"Did you hear?"

"Yes. It was the church. I take it not too much damage was done."

"No. Praise God for that. I just don't understand this person, Nate."

"Neither do I, my love. We will eventually catch the person. Let's just trust God's timing for this. Now, let's go fix breakfast and get some work done. How about it?"

After breakfast Nate went to do some outside chores and Carrie was making her third loaf of bread when the telephone rang again. Her heart gave a lurch as she remembered the earlier phone call. *Maybe Luke has more news*, she thought. *Maybe they've caught the person.*

"Hello," she said, sounding more at ease than what she actually felt.

"Maw, it's Belinda."

"Hi, Dear. Did you get any rest last night?"

"Not much, but, Maw, that's not why I'm calling. It's Lily."

"Lily? Is something wrong with Lily?"

"Yes, Maw. The doctor says she had a heart attack."

Carrie gasped for air, turning to reach for a chair.

"Maw? Are you okay?"

Carrie couldn't find her voice.

"Maw?"

Finally, Carrie spoke. "Yes, Belinda. I'm here. It just took me by surprise. Tell me everything."

"Well, Mary Carlisle called just a few minutes ago. She said they were eating breakfast—she, Lily, and Sarah—when Lily just grabbed her chest, cried out and started gasping for breath. If she and Sarah had not reached her in time, she would have fallen from her chair. They called Doc White, and he came in just minutes. He said it was definitely a heart attack."

"Where is she?"

"She's in her room at the boarding house. Mary took the day off to stay with her."

"I'll come just as soon as I can find Nate and get ready," said Carrie.

"She's resting comfortably now, Maw, so don't hurry."

"Thank you, Belinda. I'll see you in a bit."

An hour later Carrie and Nate arrived at the boarding house.

Sarah McLindy greeted them. "Good morning. I'm so sorry about Lily, but she is going to be all right. Doc White got here in plenty of time. He gave her some medicine, and she is resting quite comfortably now. Mary won't leave her side."

Carrie was surprised at Lily's paleness as she entered her room. Lily had always been robust, and this was not the sister she was used to seeing. She walked to her bedside and took her hand. Mary sat in a chair on the other side of the bed.

"She's been asleep for the past three hours. Doc said that is best for her right now."

"I just couldn't believe my ears when Belinda called," said Carrie in a low voice. "Lily has always been so healthy."

"I'm still healthy."

As Carrie and Mary looked back at the bed, Lily was trying to sit up.

"No, no, Lily," said Mary. "Doc says you must lie still and rest."

"I'm just trying to move this old body a bit," said Lily. "All this flab has to move now and then. Sister, what on earth are you doing here. Can't a woman have a bad day without everyone showing up?"

Though she tried to sound rough, Carrie could hear the uncertainty in her voice.

"They said you had a heart attack, but I knew you were just vying for attention," laughed Carrie, trying to go along with Lily's carefree attitude.

Before Lily could make a retort, Doc White came in.

"Good morning, Carrie, Mary. How is our patient?"

"Just ask the patient, Doc," said Lily. "I ain't six feet under yet."

"Well, if you don't start taking your medicine I prescribed months ago, you will be," retorted Doc.

"Doc..." said Lily, a warning in her voice.

"Medicine? What medicine?" queried Carrie.

"Yes," echoed Mary, "what medicine?"

"Doc..." said Lily again.

"Don't 'Doc' me," he said irascibly.

Turning to Carrie and Mary he said, "I prescribed medicine for her heart condition almost a year ago, and here I find she's not been taking it. No wonder she had a heart attack. Why come to me, if you don't do what I tell you?"

"What heart condition, Doc?" asked Carrie. "I've never heard anything about a heart condition."

"Doc..." said Lily, almost pleading this time.

Doc White ignored her. "Lily has had a weak heart for some time: several years, I would say. I prescribed medicine to help with the rhythm and nitroglycerin pills for such times as this morning, and then I found out she never even had the prescription filled."

"Lily!" gasped Carrie. "Why?"

"Oh, my heart just acts up every now and then. Nothing to get my bloomers in a twist over. I didn't need any old pills."

"I think this morning told you otherwise," said Doc, eyebrows arching.

"She *will* get the prescription filled, and she *will* take them from now on, won't you, Lily?" said Carrie, a stern look on her face.

"Yeah, yeah," answered Lily. "I'll follow Doc's orders, Sister Drill Sergeant."

At this, Mary began to giggle. Carrie couldn't help but join in, and soon Lily was laughing, too. Only Doc kept a stern countenance, but looked like it could give way to laughter at any minute.

"I'll go now," he said. "I have other patients who want to follow my orders. I'll be back tomorrow, unless I'm needed sooner. You are *not* to get out of that bed, Lily Tyler, except to use the john. Understand?"

"Yes, Doc," answered Lily, as meekly as she could manage.

Doctor White took his leave, and Carrie sat down in a chair beside Lily's bed.

"Lily, why didn't you tell any of us about your heart condition? Don't you know we care about you?"

"It wasn't that," answered Lily. "I guess I just thought if I didn't mention it, maybe it would go away. Besides, I deserve it for all the wrongs I've done in my life."

"Don't talk that way, Lily," said Carrie. "You have been forgiven for those things, and you've done a lot of good for people in the last years."

"Nothing can make up for the hurt I caused," replied Lily, shaking her head. "Some things just can't be smoothed over."

Carrie looked over at Mary, to find her face completely ashen. She realized Mary knew nothing of what Lily was talking about. She decided to change the subject.

"Do you know what brought on the attack, Lily?"

Lily hesitated a moment before answering.

"I think at first it was the siren. That piercing sound in the middle of the night, just sent chills through me. I kept wondering what could be on fire this time. Then..."

"Then what?" asked Carrie, when Lily seemed reluctant to continue.

"Then when they said it was the church..."

Lily wiped at a tear. "I just couldn't stand the thought of Homer losing the church. It means everything to him, and he's been through so much in his life. It was just more than my old heart could bear. I've hurt him enough myself. He doesn't deserve more hurt."

"Homer has forgiven you, Lily. You know that."

"But it doesn't undo the hurt I caused him," said Lily.

The look of pain and sadness on her face tore at Carrie's heart.

Lily continued. "To beat it all, he showed up here this morning wanting me to come stay with him and Trula until I'm well. Can you beat that?"

Carrie smiled and rubbed her sister's hand. "That's what forgiveness is all about, Lily. You just need to learn to accept the forgiveness. We can never go forward while we're looking back. You need, most of all, to forgive yourself and look to the future—and take your medicine, so you'll *have* a future!"

Silence filled the room for a few minutes, as each tried to cope with their thoughts. Mary sat looking perplexed, but Carrie felt if anyone told her the story it should be Lily. Mary finally spoke.

"So you think the fire at the church caused your heart attack, Lily?" she asked.

"Oh, I don't know," replied Lily. "I guess the attack was just waiting to happen."

"You know you are welcome to come stay with Nate and me," offered Carrie.

Lily wiped another stray tear. "Thank you, Sister, from the bottom of my heart, but I would like to try to stay here, if I can work it out. Mary has to go back to work and Sarah has her hands full running the boarding house. If I have to, I will go stay with Homer and Trula, but I really would like to just stay here."

"Then I'm sure we can work things out," affirmed Carrie. "We can arrange for someone to check in on you several times during the day until you are up and around."

"All taken care of!" said a voice from the doorway. Syrena walked in with a bright smile shaping her face and the glow that emanated only from mothers-to-be. Carrie realized they hadn't told anyone the news yet, and made a mental reminder to keep quiet.

"What's taken care of?" asked Lily. "Oh, good to see you, Syrena."

"And it's good to see you, Lily. Everything is taken care of. We have someone to come by three or four times a day for the next week or so to check on you, get you to the bathroom, help with your bath, and see that you take your medicine to help you rest."

"That's wonderful, Syrena," said Carrie. "You have been a busy young lady. See, Lily, how people love you!"

"Who's giving up their time for the likes of me?" asked Lily, her voice filled with emotion she tried to hide.

"Well, the first one to volunteer was Mrs. Ilson," answered Syrena. "What do you think of that?"

"But she doesn't even know me," replied Lily.

"I think she wants to feel useful and a part of the community. She asked to come Mondays and Wednesdays. We know she will be a good caregiver. Look what she did for Matthew."

"Who else has lost their mind?" Lily was trying to hide her feelings, but her success was questionable.

125

"On Tuesdays, Belinda and I will take different parts of the day. Trula will come on Thursdays, and...I thought Carrie might come on Fridays. Right, Maw Carrie?"

"I would be glad to," answered Carrie. "What about weekends?"

"I can help then," offered Mary, eagerness in her voice.

"Well, I was hoping you and Sarah might keep check on her at night," said Syrena, "but if you would like to do it on Sundays, it would be greatly appreciated. I think you could do that and still go to church. Ady Rose and Cindy have volunteered to do Saturdays."

"Great day! You've got everybody in the countryside taking care of me!" laughed Lily. "I won't have any secrets left!"

"It will only be for a week or so," said Mary. "If I know you, you will be back on your feet in no time."

"Get this..." whispered Syrena, in a conspiratorial voice, "Floyd volunteered to come and help anytime we need him!"

With this they all broke into laughter.

"Now you've done it, girls," said Lily. "That was too much laughter. Someone get me to the bathroom!"

CHAPTER 16

Samuel came home on Monday. His cheeks had more color in them and he was able to take two or three steps with his braces and crutches, an improvement for which they were all thankful, but he was not even close to being well. He was, however, excited to be home and back with his family. Carrie immediately noticed Amanda's fatigue.

"Amanda, it must have been so hard on you, all the way down there without Jessie, and caring for Samuel nonstop."

"I must admit," said Amanda, with a slight nod, "I am pretty tired. They were good to us and I met many nice folks, but I missed my family and just being where I knew everyone. I think, too, that I'm a little disappointed. I guess I expected more progress than this, although they had warned us not to expect too much the first time."

"I think you'll see a big difference the next time," soothed Carrie. "We are just so blessed that the polio hasn't affected him worse than what it has. I do believe he'll walk again, Amanda. In the meantime, you need to get some rest. I will be here first thing tomorrow to take care of Samuel while you get out for a little while, and I won't take no for an answer."

Amanda stifled a yawn. "I won't turn down your offer, Maw Carrie. It will be good to get some fresh air and just to sit down and rest for a few hours. What's this I hear about Lily having a heart attack?"

Carrie nodded. "I'm afraid you heard right. I'm on my way to check on her now. She's trying to put up a front, but she doesn't look at all well."

Carrie left Amanda and the children and went on toward the boarding house. As she was going in, she met Floyd coming out. He had a somber look on his usually happy face.

Greeting him, Carrie asked, "Is Lily worse, Floyd?"

"No, not worse. I just think her heart problem is worse than she lets on. She thinks laughing about the matter will make it go away, but that's not being realistic, Mrs. Carrie. I'm a might afraid she won't take care of herself. I tried to persuade her to marry me and I could take care of her, but she's a stubborn woman."

"That she is," laughed Carrie. "You're a good man Floyd. Very few men would care that much."

"No, Miss Carrie, I'm not a good man," said Floyd. Then he walked away.

Carrie stood there for a minute, puzzled by his remark. *What could he have meant by that?*

Finding no answer, she went on in to see Lily. Sarah McLindy was coming from her room with a tray in her hand.

"Good day to you, Carrie. Coming to check up on that sister of yours? I love her dearly, but she can be contrary. I told her Rome wasn't built in a day, but she says she's nowhere near as big as Rome and doesn't need near as much fixing."

Carrie laughed and shook her head as she entered the room.

"Good morning, Lily. Are you being a good patient or a contrary one?"

"I don't need to be any kind," said Lily, flinging her hand in the air. "You'd think I was a hundred years old and bedridden, the way people want to fuss over me. I need to be up out of this bed and doing for myself. All this fuss is going to cause me to have another heart attack."

"Simmer down," Carrie reprimanded her sister. "We're all just trying to help you. You'll be well again in no time, if you'll just follow Doc's orders."

"I need to be up and about, helping Sarah with this boarding house. She's going to wear herself down, and on top of that, she's trying to wait on me. Meals in bed! Never heard of so much folderol!"

The room was quiet for a moment, as Carrie gave no response. Then Lily spoke again, this time more quietly.

"Carrie, why would anyone want to burn down the church? Homer has never hurt anyone, and he works so hard for the folks around here. Who would do such a thing?"

"I don't know why they've set any of the fires," answered Carrie. "I first thought someone had something against our family, but now I just don't know. The school has nothing to do with our family."

"Well, Cindy and Landon work there," offered Lily. "Could that be the connection?"

Carrie pondered the thought for a moment. "I suppose that's possible, but what has our family ever done to hurt anyone? If Tom was still alive, I might understand someone with a vendetta against him. He hurt many people. But he's been gone for years."

"There's an old saying," said Lily, "about the bad that men do living on after them. God knows, me and Tom caused hurt for a lot of people, but why would they want to blame you or Luke or Homer? I just don't understand it."

"Let's just pray they find this person soon," said Carrie.

After leaving Lily, Carrie went on over to the dress shop where she and some of the women of the town were going to get started on the baseball shirts. The town had found a new reason to be excited again, with the plans in full swing for a baseball team. Sile J. had already begun practice with the kids, both boys and girls.

Making her way down the street, she heard someone call her name. It was Luke and young Jacob.

"Maw, wait up!"

She stood waiting while they caught up with her.

"I've got some good news, Maw. We just received a telephone call from Herb Moore on the town council. Richmond has agreed to fund the building of the new school. We can begin any time!"

"Oh, Hallelujah!" cried Carrie. "That is wonderful news. The kids will have a school, and Landon and the other teachers will have a job. Come on with me and tell Belinda and the others."

As they entered the dress shop, Belinda, Nettie, and four other women from the town were cutting cloth. They were all thrilled with the news.

"See there," said Nettie, with an emphatic nod of her head. "We have tons of things to be thankful for: a new ball team, Anja's parents coming from Belgium, and now we're going to have us a brand new schoolhouse. Now, ain't that something to just crow about?"

They all laughed.

"I couldn't have said it better, Nettie," laughed Belinda.

"Now if they could just find this fire culprit," said Mattie McClain. "Sure don't want to see the new school burn."

"Don't even say such a thing, Mattie McClain," gasped Nora Wilson.

"Well, you never know."

"I feel sure they'll catch him soon," offered Luke. "Look at this last time. The watch team saw the fire before it could do much damage. We're getting closer."

"Closer to what?" asked Mary Carlisle, coming into the room.

"Catching this mad hatter who's burning up everything in sight," retorted Mattie.

"We can only hope," replied Mary, picking up her scissors.

Carrie worked until four o'clock and then hurried home, anxious to tell Nate about the funding for the school.

The next day Nate walked to town with her. He needed some things from the hardware store, and Carrie was going to spend the day taking care of Samuel.

"Good morning, Samuel!" she called as she walked into his bedroom.

Samuel's eyes lit up somewhat, but Carrie could tell he was a sad little boy.

She plopped her bag down next to him. "I brought my checker board with me. I feel sure I can beat you a few games. What do you think?"

"Okay," he answered listlessly, not at all excited.

Digging into her bag, she added, "I also had some peanut butter cookies I thought a young man I know might like. I even have enough for Benjamin and Ivey."

"They're out playing baseball," said Samuel, and Carrie could see the tears in his eyes. "They're out with Uncle Sile."

Uh-oh, thought Carrie, *someone is a little bit jealous. He's having to share his Uncle Sile. Give me the right words, Lord.*

"You know, Samuel, Uncle Sile missed you so much while you were gone. He thought and thought of ways he could make you feel better when you came home. I think he wanted to get this ball team together so you would have something to watch."

"Really?" asked Samuel, his eyes widening.

"Really. Benjamin and Ivey missed you, too, and they needed something to keep them from being so sad. Now, why don't we play a game of checkers before your warm water bath?"

Thirty minutes and two games later, Samuel was tired of checkers and it was time for the warm bath. As Carrie rose to go carry the water, the front door opened.

"Am I in time?"

It was Sile J.

"In time for what?" asked Carrie.

"I came to give my favorite boy his warm bath treatment! After all, I need to tell him about the ball team and get his advice on a few things."

Carrie had never seen a face light up as quickly.

"You need my advice, Uncle Sile?"

"I most certainly do, Samuel J. I also need to know what you think of the new baseball shirts."

Sile J. opened up the shirt he had brought and turned it to the back. There, in large red letters was the name: Samuel's Warriors!

Samuel stared in amazement.

"What do you think?" asked Sile J.

For a moment Samuel continued to stare, and then he said, "I think this is about the best surprise I've ever had."

"Then I take it you approve. 'Cause we can change it if you don't like it," said Sile J.

Gathering all his strength, Samuel answered, "No, Uncle Sile, don't change a thing."

At the supper table that night, Nate laughed as Carrie recanted the happenings of the day. "I can't wait 'til that boy can run and play baseball with the rest of the kids. It will be a sight to see."

By mid-August Samuel was taking several steps and was attending all the ballgames. Jessie had bought a wheelchair to help him get outside more, and Sile J. had fixed him a special place to sit and watch the games.

He really got into the games and you could hear him yelling, "Run, Benjamin! Hurry! Aw, ump, he was safe! That was a ball, not a strike!"

It was time, to everyone's regret, for Samuel and Amanda to go back to Warm Springs for another month of treatments. While they looked forward to more improvement, it was hard for Jessie and Amanda to see their family go in all different directions. There was a bright spot, however. At Cammy's request and Belinda's and Joe's approval, Cammy was going with Amanda and Samuel this time, to help ease the work for Amanda and just be company for both of them. The new school, though coming along well, would not be finished before mid-September, so school would start later than usual. Cammy would return in plenty of time. She had packed lots of books to read to Samuel, and she looked forward to introducing him to *Treasure Island* and *Black Beauty*.

Jessie left on Wednesday to take them to Warm Springs and planned to return on Friday. Beady and John would take care of things while he was away. Lily was doing much better, even doing light work at the boarding house. Syrena was blossoming as a mother-in-waiting should, and all seemed well in the little mountain community. On Friday, there was some unexpected but happy news as Nettie walked into the dress shop. Carrie was there helping with some extra sewing, since she didn't need to help with Lily anymore.

"Well, ladies," called Nettie, "hold on to your bloomers, 'cause this gal has an announcement to make."

They all stopped their work and turned to hear what she had to say.

"After dating that thick-skulled Carl Hamons for nigh on ten years, he finally broke down and asked me to marry him. Ladies, you are looking at an engaged middle-aged woman."

Their mouths fell open as their minds digested the news. Carl Hamons was a good man who owned a farm on the Willow Creek section of the community. He also ran a grist mill. He and Nettie had been dating for years, and by now most of the folks of the area had given up on a marriage between the two.

Finding her breath, Belinda crossed the room and hugged Nettie. "Thirty-eight is not middle-aged, and I hope that man knows just how lucky he is. I'm happy for you, Nettie."

"Well," replied Nettie, not cracking a smile, "he should know it. I tell him all the time."

Carrie and Mary rose to give her a hug.

"When is the big event?" asked Mary, being polite but showing little enthusiasm.

"Two weeks from this Saturday. "Don't want to give him too long to think about it."

"Where are you getting married?" asked Belinda. "You are welcome to use the hotel, you know."

"Weell..." began Nettie. "Carl really wants to get married in a church."

"That's a wonderful idea," said Carrie. "Now, what can we do to help?"

"I don't rightly know," Nettie replied. "We just want a small wedding, with family and a few close friends like you all—no big shebang, or anything like that. You know my family. They wouldn't know how to act at a big wedding, and sorry as some of them are, they're still my family."

"What can we do to help?" ask Belinda, repeating Carrie's question.

"You can help me plan it all," answered Nettie. "This is not exactly my forte, you know. I just want to make sure it's simple. Nothing fancy. You know Carl; he'd be like a banny hen in a cattle stampede."

"And just what would that be like?" asked Carrie, laughing at Nettie's expression.

"Well, it wouldn't be purty," replied Nettie.

"What about a dress, Nettie?" Mary finally joined the conversation. "Could we help you make a dress?"

Nettie nodded. "I would like a new dress: white and simple, something I can wear again to a party or to church. I'm not going to have bridesmaids and all that, but I'd be mighty pleased, Miss Belinda, if you'd stand up with me, as sort of an unofficial maid-of-honor. Carl's gonna ask his brother Charlie to stand up for him. Carl says he'll wear a suit, but ain't no way he'll get Charlie in one. We'll do good to talk him out of bibbed overalls."

"I think all of that will be just fine, Nettie," said Carrie. "I think a wedding should be just what the bride and groom want it to be."

Nettie looked over at Mary, a serious look shading her eyes.

"Mary, you haven't been here long enough to know much about me and my family. I love my family, but there's no denying some have done some bad things in their lives. I won't go into that, but when most people were turning up their noses at me, Belinda gave me a chance, and I've tried never to let her down. I was determined not to walk down that road my mother and sisters have walked. I owe more than I could ever repay to Belinda and Miss Carrie and all their family. They just took me in and made me one of them."

"They have a way of doing that," nodded Mary. "Thank you, Nettie, for telling me that. I'm sure not one to judge, and I value your friendship deeply."

"Now, about that dress…" said Belinda, changing back to lighter conversation. "I have some white cloth left over from another wedding. Let me go get it. Do you know what style you want?"

Talk then turned to dress styles, receptions, and all those things a bride-to-be needs to talk about.

Two weeks later, Nettie and Carl were married by Homer in the little Missionary Baptist Church that had been saved from an awful fire. As she had no father, Joe gave the bride away. Nettie was a lovely bride in her new white dress. As a surprise, Belinda had made a little wreath of white flowers for her hair, and Syrena had made a bouquet of yellow roses and white daisies. Carrie gave her a small necklace of pearls for her "something old." The forty-six-year-old groom smiled like a schoolboy, and after a great deal of persuasion, Charlie gave up the bibbed overalls for one day. He even had a new haircut and shave to show off with dress pants and a white shirt. Matildy Willis was getting up in years now, but she showed up at the wedding with a new store-bought dress and a face glowing with happiness and pride for her daughter. It was a beautiful ceremony, followed by a reception at the hotel. Nettie's family, scorned by some in the town, joined with those who live truly by God's Word, and had a marvelous time.

CHAPTER 17

The following day, a Sunday, found the people back in church. Nettie and Carl had gone to Kentucky for a brief honeymoon, as Carl couldn't be away from the farm for too long. Nettie would still work two days a week in the dress shop, but the rest of her time would be needed in her new home on the farm. Carrie was pleased to see that Nettie's mother and three of Nettie's sisters had come to church for the first time. Among them were Lizzie Hankins and her husband Henry. Lizzie and Henry had been neighbors of Carrie's for years, moving in across the creek back when Tom was still alive. It was a little awkward at first, especially for Tom, since Lizzie had once been his "lady friend", but Lizzie had changed from the woman she once was.

The sound of the piano signaled that it was time for the chatter and fellowship to end.

"Good morning," Pastor Homer greeted the little congregation. "God is good all the time..."

"All the time God is good!" quoted the congregation.

"I would like to welcome my mother, Lily Tyler, back to church today," said Homer. "She is still very weak, but God has been good to heal her, and we praise Him for that."

At this, everyone applauded, and Lily blushed and waved her hand.

They sang a couple of songs, and then Homer began his sermon. About five minutes into the sermon, Benjamin suddenly stood up and yelled, "The orphanage!"

Homer stopped in mid-sentence, and everyone stared at Benjamin.

"The orphanage!" he yelled again, pointing out the window. At the same time the fire siren screamed.

As everyone looked, Charles shouted, "The orphanage is on fire!"

Everyone scrambled to get outside. The orphanage was definitely in flames. Both men and women worked in their Sunday best to extinguish the fire, with the Haymaker fire brigade taking the lead. Those unable to help stood sadly, shaking their heads. Some joined hands and prayed. Carrie looked around the crowd for Lily, concerned about what this could do to her. She saw her sister still standing on the church steps, looking completely distraught. Carrie hurried to her.

"Lily, are you all right?"

Tears poured down Lily's face. "Why, Carrie? Why? Oh, my sweet baby!"

Carrie knew she was referring to Alice. They sat down on the church steps, and Carrie held her sister while she sobbed.

"We can't lose Alice's Hope!" cried Lily. "Oh, please God, let them get the fire put out."

Carrie knew of nothing to say. Words would not come. She simply held Lily and watched her friends and neighbors try to save the orphanage. As she watched the frenzied crowd, she saw Nate coming toward them.

"Carrie, have you seen Floyd?"

"No, why?"

"He wasn't at church, and Nathan said he was still at the orphanage when they all left for church. We're afraid he might still be in there."

"Oh, no!" moaned Lily.

"Now we don't know that, Lily," said Nate. "We just can't find him. I'm going back to help, unless you need me here."

"No," said Carrie. "You go on, but please be careful, Nate."

As she watched him go, she whispered a prayer.

She turned to check on Lily, but as she did she saw Floyd coming toward them, fear written all over his face.

"Are you okay, Lily?" he called before he reached the steps.

"Am I okay? What about you? They're looking all over for you!"

Carrie saw Ethan in the crowd just in front of them and called to him. Thankfully he heard her and came running.

"Ethan, find Grandpa Nate, and tell him Floyd is all right and is with us at the church. If you can't find Nate, tell one of the other men."

"Okay, Grandma Carrie!" he called as he ran toward the men working to put out the fire.

"Floyd, where have you been?" asked Carrie.

For a moment Floyd's face reddened. "Well, I didn't go to church this morning because I was going to go over to the boarding house and stay with Lily. When I got there Freddy Ware, one of the boarders, said he saw Lily and Sarah headed to church. It was a little late for me to come on, so I just stayed and jawed with Freddy for a while. Then I heard the fire siren. Lily, are you okay?"

Before she could answer, Nate returned. "Floyd, I sure am glad to see you. You gave us quite a scare."

"Sorry 'bout that," said Floyd. "I was at the boarding house. How bad is it, Nate?"

Nate looked over at Lily, then shook his head. As he did that, Lily looked up and caught the motion. She gave a pitiful moan.

"Alice's Hope is gone. My baby's dream of a place to love unwanted children is *gone*. I can't bear the...oh..."

Lily grabbed her chest and fell over against Carrie.

"I'll find the doctor," called Nate, as he ran into the crowd.

"Lily! Lily! Speak to me!" called Floyd. "Forgive me, Lily!" But Lily had fainted.

Though it seemed like hours, Doc White arrived in just minutes. Two men followed with a stretcher.

Placing a nitroglycerin pill under her tongue, he said, "Let's get her over to the boarding house, and fast."

Sarah McLindy was standing outside her boarding house watching the men fight the fire. When she saw them coming with Lily, she led the way to Lily's room. The men lifted her into her bed and then left. Doc gave her an injection, then turned to Carrie and Sarah.

"She most likely won't wake up for a while. The shock was just too much for her."

Carrie looked into Doc's eyes. "But she *will* wake up, won't she?"

Doc dipped his head. "That's up to the Lord, Carrie. More than that, I can't tell you."

Floyd left after a few moments, to go check on the damage of the fire. Carrie couldn't help but notice the smell of smoke as he bent to kiss Lily's cheek.

She sat down and just watched her sister sleeping. *Please, Lord,* her heart whispered, *please help my sister. I've forgiven her everything, and I know you have, too. I don't know your plans here, but I ask you to be merciful and give her peace and comfort.*

As she sat there deep in memories, she heard someone come into the room.

"Is she all right?"

It was Mary.

"I don't know, Mary. At least she is resting."

"Did the fire bring on all of this?"

"Yes, I think so. Alice's Hope was everything to her. Did she ever tell you its story?"

"No. I know it meant a great deal to her, but Lily was private about a lot of things."

"Alice was her daughter, one of the children she gave away. Alice came back later...there's a long story there, but to make it short, they made their peace. Lily took care of her in her last days. Alice was raised in an orphanage, but not a good one. It was her dream to build an orphanage where children could be valued, loved, and educated. She lived just long enough to see her dream come true. When it burned today, I think it literally broke Lily's heart. It was like losing Alice all over again."

Mary sat for a long time in silence. "Some things are just never what they seem, are they?" she finally said.

Carrie gave no answer. In fact, she knew of no answer for that question. It seemed to have meaning that lay hidden in Mary's past. Mary Carlisle was a complex young woman.

Nate arrived later, and just behind him were Luke and Homer. Carrie looked at him, a question in her eyes, to which he sadly shook his head.

"Completely gone?" she whispered.

Nate nodded, "I'm afraid so."

Carrie shook her head sadly as her heart cried out, *How will Lily survive this? And it's not just Lily, God. What will this do to Luke?*

She looked at Nate, for the first time seeing his anguish. She took his hand. "All of you did your best, Nate."

He nodded but did not reply.

As they sat in silence, Luke whispered, "How is she, Maw?"

"Not good, son."

"Right now I would just like to get my hands on the person who did this," said Luke through gritted teeth. "This person couldn't have a heart."

Carrie didn't even try to calm him, because her feelings echoed his right now. It had been a long time since she had felt such anger.

"I think right now even God is angry." The three turned to look at Homer. It was unusual for him to speak this way.

Carrie went to him and put her arms around him. "God will work all of this out, Homer. I don't know how right now, but I trust Him."

"I trust him, too, Aunt Carrie, and I know He will work this out for good, but I think we all have to have just a moment of anger for these terrible deeds. We need to find this person soon."

"Doctor White says Lily won't wake up for several hours, Homer."

"I know. Trula will sit with her tonight, Aunt Carrie. You need some rest, and I need to be out there pastoring my flock. As soon as Lily is well enough, we will take her to our home and care for her."

It was almost two days before Lily finally awakened. She was extremely weak.

"Orphanage?"

This was her first word.

"Well, just look at you Mother Lily," said Trula. "Did you finally decide to join the land of the living?"

"Wasn't my decision!" said Lily, with a mixture of sadness and anger. "Don't have much left here anymore."

Trula wiped the hair from Lily's face. "You have many here who love you."

"Is Alice's Hope completely gone?" asked Lily. "Did I just dream it?"

"I'm afraid it was no dream," replied Trula. "I wish it was. But, Lily, we'll find a way to build it back. I promise you that."

Lily did not respond. The silence was broken when the door opened and Doc White and Carrie entered the room.

"How is my most contrary patient today?" asked Doc White. "I see you finally got your nap over."

He felt her forehead and took her heartbeat. "Well, the two-day nap seems to have done some good. The heart rate is better and not so shallow."

"Is that supposed to be good news?" asked Lily grumpily.

"Why, Lily, of course it's good news," said Carrie. "It means God still has work for you here."

"What could an old, sorry, useless thing like me have left to do?" asked Lily, still in a grumpy mood.

"I guess you'll just have to ask God," laughed Carrie lightly.

"When can we take her to our house, Doc?" asked Trula.

"Who said I was going to your house?" asked Lily. "I ain't so bad off I can't make my own decisions."

"Well, they definitely aren't taking you there because of your sweetness!" growled Doc White.

At this, Trula gasped and they all stared at the doctor. Then Lily began to laugh. It was weak, but it was laughter. Then Doc began to laugh and Carrie and Trula joined in.

"You don't pull any punches, Doc," laughed Lily. "I guess that's what I always liked about you. Dent always said you can trust a man who tells it like it is."

"Are you finally admitting you like me, Lily?" asked Doc. "This is certainly a day to write down in my journal. Miracles do still happen."

"That was a moment of weakness," said Lily. "I did just have a heart attack, you know. I can't be held responsible for the things I say—and don't you dare write that down anywhere!"

"I think I might just resort to blackmail," said Doc White, a twinkle in his eye. "I won't write anything down that you say *if* you mind what I say."

"That's deep down and dirty, you old codger," growled Lily. "Okay, you got me. What do I have to do?"

Doc White, looking at his papers, seemed to ponder before answering. "I think you need to stay here another week. Then, if you are able to be moved, I think you need to take Homer and Trula up on their offer. You

140

are not going to bounce back from this attack as soon as you did the last one. You'll need some care."

Lily nodded. "Like I said, you tell it like it is. So, Doc—am I going to be bedfast? Are you saying I'm too old and my heart is too worn out to get better?"

"Did I say that, Lily Tyler? Are you the doctor now? The truth is, I don't know how well you will recover. We just have to wait and see. You're just contrary enough to outlive me."

"Well, I may just aim for that!" said Lily, with a shake of her head and a loud "humph."

In another week, Lily was able to go live with Homer and Trula. She was not happy about the situation, but remembered her agreement with Doc White.

"This is going to make it too hard on you and Trula," she complained to Homer.

He looked at his mother a few minutes, as if choosing carefully the words he wanted to say. "Mother, do you remember what you said to Alice when you wanted her to come stay with you? I don't remember the exact words, but I think you said something about making up for the past, getting to know each other and getting to really talk to each other. Well, that's what I want now, a chance for us to really get to know each other."

Lily was silent for a moment, a tear sliding down her cheek. Then she looked into her son's eyes.

"You called me 'mother'," she said.

The little town of Haymaker was busy in the next few weeks. The remains of the orphanage had to be cleaned up, and places had to be found for all the children. Some were placed temporarily in homes around the area. Nathan and Lissa took three home with them. They were renting a little house at the edge of town. The others had to be moved to the orphanage over in Ryland. It was a sad time for all of them. In the meantime, Nathan helped his dad on the farm and Lissa took care of the children. They were hoping to get enough from the insurance on the orphanage to at least begin building it back.

Jessie was also busy. He had to find out who was setting the fires. The people were scared, and when a town gets scared, it can do some dangerous things. People were demanding answers, and Jessie had none. He had asked Homer to make a list of all his church members who weren't in church that Sunday, and he did likewise with the Primitive Baptist Church and the Methodist Church. That should narrow the suspect list substantially. If they were in church, they could not have set the fire; if they were not in church, they would have to give an accounting of their whereabouts that morning. Proving the word of the absentees would be the hard part. It was a start, at least. The watch teams were working extra hard, and several more had joined the teams.

Almost one month after the fire, Samuel, Amanda, and Cammy came home. It was time for school to start. The news was not what Jessie and Amanda had hoped for. Samuel was walking well with his braces and crutches now, and could go wherever he pleased without help, except on steps. The doctors had given them no hope of further improvement. It was unlikely he would ever be able to walk without the braces and crutches. On the brighter side, he would not be bedfast and he had no breathing problems. The question they faced now was whether or not he could go to school. They had asked Landon to come to the house to talk to them and Samuel.

After he had listened to Jessie's and Amanda's concerns, he looked at Samuel. "I think the first thing I need to know is this: Samuel, do you want to go to school?"

"Yes!" answered Samuel, nodding his head enthusiastically. "More than anything right now."

"Can you handle not being able to run and play with the other children?" asked Landon.

"Yes," replied Samuel, just a hint of sadness in his face. "I wish I could, but I know I'll never be able to do that anymore."

"Samuel!" gasped his mother. "You can't lose hope!"

"But the man explained it to me," said Samuel.

"Man? What man?" asked Jessie.

"The man I saw one night in my dream."

Jessie and Amanda looked at each other, confusion covering their face. Landon asked, "What did the man look like, Samuel?"

"Well, I'm pretty sure it was God. He was sort of like a man, but he was hard to see because he had a bright light all around him—sort of like it was coming from inside of him."

"Were you afraid?" asked Landon.

Jessie and Amanda sat in stunned silence.

"Not one bit," answered Samuel. "He had a kind voice, and he called me by my name, so I knew that he knew me."

"What did he say? Do you remember?"

"Oh, I remember it *real* well," replied Samuel. "He told me he had big plans for me, but I would have to wear the braces and probably use my crutches so I could carry out his plans."

"Did he say what those plans are?"

"No. He said I just had to trust him and be strong, and little by little, he would show me what he wanted me to do. I asked him why I had to wear braces to do it, but he just said he would show me. Then he said, 'Be strong, Samuel. Be strong.' I told him I would."

They all sat in silence. Then Samuel asked, "Don't you believe me?"

Jessie knelt by his young son. "Of course we believe you. I guess we are just taken by surprise. Samuel do you think you can manage the steps at school? What will you do while the other children are playing?"

"I know I can manage at school, Papa," he answered. "I know Benjamin and Ivey and Christopher and Jacob will help me...and probably most of the other kids. I don't know what I'll do while they are playing, but I suppose that's one of the things the man will show me. I really like to read, so maybe I can do that."

Jessie, Amanda and Landon looked at each other, amazement in their eyes.

"You know, Samuel," said Landon finally. "I'm totally convinced you can handle school. I'll be looking for you day-after-tomorrow."

CHAPTER 18

Homer and Trula devotedly cared for Lily, but she wasn't recovering like before. Some days she could sit up for a few minutes, but most of the time she remained in bed. They were seeing fewer and fewer of her "spunky" days. She sent for Carrie to come see her.

"Sister," she said, the day Carrie came, "I got some things I need to get off my chest. I ain't gonna be here much longer, and I'm not sad about that, but I need to say some things."

"Lily, you don't need to tell me anything," said Carrie. "You and I cleared up everything between us a long time ago. You are not the person you used to be."

"I know that," said Lily, "but I just need to say some things, maybe for me more than for you. Okay?"

"Yes," answered Carrie. "Yes, Lily, it's okay."

Lily took a minute to compose her thoughts.

"I did a lot of things for spite, Sis. You and Nora were always so good, and I resented you for that. Seems like I always had the ole devil in me, just nipping at my heels all the time."

Carrie started to speak, but Lily held up her hand.

"I had my eyes on Tom long before you did. I seemed to always like those 'show-offey' men, and Tom was pure show-off. Then he got his eyes on you, and I couldn't stand that. I did anything I could to get his attention away from you. When I told him I was pregnant, he denied it was his. That's when I married Reed. I married him to spite Tom, and because I needed a father for my baby."

"Didn't Reed know he wasn't the father?" asked Carrie.

"No. I'm ashamed to tell you now, but I had been with both of them. He never knew, until several years later. I was tired of putting up with him and I wanted out of the marriage. He wouldn't agree to it, so out of spite, I told him Tiny Alice was Tom's. He left, and I never saw him again. I still saw Tom from time to time, even after I married Reed."

Lily paused to rest a moment as she searched Carrie's face for reaction.

"I gave my little children away for spite. Reed was always harping about me being a bad mother, and his maw was always belittling everything I did. After Reed left, I started seeing Dent. Well, truth be told, I was seeing him and Tom both before Reed ever left. I decided to get even with Reed, but especially his parents. So I came up with the notion of giving my kids away. I wasn't a good mother. I didn't even have the feelings for my children that a mother ought to have. The only feeling I had the day they got on that train was the feeling of triumph over everyone who tried to talk me out of it. I was going to start over, and I was going to have myself a life. Can you believe anyone could be so callous, Carrie? Like I said, I had the pure ole devil in me, and I didn't care who I hurt."

Carrie sat silently, completely unable to answer.

Lily continued. "I didn't see Tom anymore after I married Dent. That doesn't mean I didn't see other men, but not Tom. Lord, Carrie, I was a mean sinful woman. How God could forgive me, I will never know. I think the first time I ever felt love in my heart for anyone was when Alice came back here, and I had to tell her the truth so she wouldn't marry Luke. I didn't do that for spite. I hated myself and all that I had done. When she told me what had happened to little James, I wanted to die. But Carrie, I loved that girl before she died, and I think she loved me."

"Yes, Lily," said Carrie, almost in a whisper. "I am positive Alice forgave you and loved you. She was that kind of woman."

"God must have surely had his hand on her," said Lily, "to make her the precious woman she was after having a mother like me. Look at Homer.

God definitely had his hand on him, and Carrie, he actually loves me. Can you believe that?"

Carrie nodded, smiling through tears. "Yes, I believe it, Lily."

"I wish I could have known Belle," Lily said. "She must have been a special young woman, too. For awhile, she was happy—and look at Cammy. She is one of the most caring, generous young ladies I know. Just goes to show, God can take something bad and make good come from it."

Lily had to rest again.

"The biggest regret I'll carry with me to my grave is James. He must have suffered terribly at that orphanage, Carrie. I'm so sorry for that. Do you think he hated me?"

"I don't know, Lily. I can't answer that."

"I just want you to know, Carrie, that if I could go back, I would never do the things I did. It makes me sick to even think about them. I love you, my dear sister."

Tears spilled from Carrie's eyes. "I love you, Lily.

"I've already talked to Homer," said Lily. "I'm leaving a letter for Cammy. Belinda will give it to her one day when the time is right. I need one more thing from you, Sis."

"What is that, Lily?"

"I want you to promise me you will do everything in your power to see that the orphanage is rebuilt. I won't be here to see it, but I can go in peace if you promise to see to it for me."

"I promise to see that it's rebuilt," agreed Carrie. "It won't be just me, though. Everyone in town will be working toward the rebuilding. It will be done."

"Do you think I could be buried in the little cemetery with Mama and Papa?"

"Of course, Lily. I promise you that."

Three days later Lily breathed her last breath, with Homer, Trula, and Doc White by her side. Homer had her funeral in the church he loved so much, and he delivered a combination eulogy and sermon about forgiveness and God's love. She would have been surprised to see the church full and overflowing. Lily was carried to the little cemetery on top of the hill where Mama Cynth and Papa Silas were buried, and they all said their final farewells. After the burial, Carrie, Nate, and her brothers remained for a while, their thoughts filled with days passed and gone.

"I remember the day we buried Mama Cynth up here," said Carrie. "It was one of the hardest things I had ever done. How she and Papa loved each other! I wonder how many babies on these hills and in the hollows she birthed. Sometimes she would birth ten or twelve in the same family. Nora and I tried to count them one time, but when we reached one hundred and thirty, we just stopped. It never mattered to Mama whether she got any pay. She just had a kind and compassionate heart like Jesus, and she wanted to help others."

"I remember the day we buried Papa and little Woody," said Sile J., standing at the foot of Woody's grave. "As hard as it was to lose Papa, burying my son was almost unbearable. Then when Lula died, I didn't think I had anything to live for, but God had more work for me to do."

"Remember how much Papa loved Woody? Those two were inseparable," said Charles.

Carrie walked to Tom's grave. "You know, Paw Charles wouldn't even allow Tom to be buried in his family cemetery. I can't blame him. You all and Eb and Will agreed to him being buried here. Seems strange to have such good buried alongside such evil."

They walked slowly back down the hillside, each lost in thoughts of yore.

Carrie remembered her promise to Lily about the orphanage, and she thought about it a great deal over the next few days. She didn't know how she would keep her promise, but she knew there would be a way.

CHAPTER 19

Almost two weeks after Lily was buried, a letter came in the mail for Carrie. Nate had gone to town for a few needed items, and returned with the letter. He sat on the porch beside her as she opened it and read:

Dear Miss Carrie,

It's been so long since I have seen you. The years have gone by quickly. I remember you with the fondest memories. You were the best woman I ever knew. My life has been good. I now have four children and twelve grandchildren. Can you believe that? One is even named after you, my youngest, Carrie Leann. She is such a good young woman, a nurse, in fact. I would love to see you, but I'm unable to travel as my lungs are so bad. Turner passed on to his reward five years ago. He was such a good husband and father. He and I took care of Mama and Rollen until they passed away. Mama's been gone twenty years now, and Rollen fourteen.

The hardest part about getting older is losing those we love.

The reason I'm writing is that I heard about the orphanage burning. I thought of you and how sad you must be. Turner left me quite well off, Miss Carrie, and I'm getting old and don't need much money to see me along. My children are doing well in their own right. I talked this over with them, and I am enclosing a check for the rebuilding of the orphanage. I hope this will make you smile. Please write to me when it's finished and tell me all about it. I'm glad you finally found happiness, because no one deserves it more. I love you very much.

Forever your friend,
Eliza Ashton

Carrie sat looking first at the letter and then at Nate. She could not believe what her eyes had read. Dear, dear Eliza. How many times she had helped Carrie when she had no one? When her babies were born, Eliza helped. When Belinda and Ady Rose were near death, she was right there by Carrie's side. She had been a true friend.

"Well, aren't you going to look at the check?" laughed Nate.

His words finally registering, Carrie unfolded the check. Her eyes widened in total disbelief.

"Fifty-thousand dollars!" she exclaimed. "Nate, it says fifty-thousand dollars! That will be plenty enough to rebuild the orphanage! Oh, I wish Lily was here to see this!"

Carrie immediately got on the phone and called Luke, Belinda, Ady Rose, Jessie, and Cindy.

"I need to see all of you right away," she said. "Can you come? Nothing is wrong. It's something good."

Within an hour, all her children were there. She first read the letter aloud, then showed them the check. They were all in disbelief as they hugged each other, squealed, and cried.

Tears rushed unchecked from Luke's eyes. "Praise God! We can rebuild Alice's Hope!"

"Each of us need to write a thank you letter to Eliza" said Cindy, ever the schoolteacher.

"I will deposit this check first thing tomorrow," said Carrie. "Shouldn't I set up a special account for this?"

"That would be best," agreed Jessie. "Maw, would you like Luke and me to go with you? Mr. Albert at the bank will be able to tell us how it should be done."

They agreed to meet at the bank at nine o'clock the next morning. Carrie slept little that night, excitement racing through her veins.

Thank you, God, her heart whispered, *for making a way to rebuild the orphanage and for giving me a way to keep my promise to Lily. Most of all, God, I thank you for giving Eliza a good life.*

She set up the account the next day with Luke, Jessie, and Joe as financial administrators in the rebuilding. Afterwards, Jessie asked Carrie and Luke to go to lunch with him.

"I need to talk to both of you," he said.

They went to Lillian's Diner and Jessie asked for a back booth.

"Is something wrong with Samuel?" asked Carrie, an eerie feeling inching its way up her spine.

"No, no," answered Jessie. "In fact, that young man amazes me daily. He gets around well, all things considered, and he never complains. I don't think I've ever seen anyone enjoy life more. The kids at school vie for the chance to help him, and Landon tells me his teachers rave about his work."

"That's a real blessing," said Luke.

Nodding, Jessie said, "The reason I wanted to talk to both of you has to do with the fires. We have narrowed the list of suspects remarkably. Two of them, though, concern me."

"Who?" asked Carrie.

"Floyd is one," answered Jessie, "and...the other is Mary Carlisle."

Carrie gasped, and Luke looked at Jessie in disbelief.

"Jessie, I don't believe it could be either of them," said Carrie. "Why do you consider them suspects?"

"Neither of them can really prove where they were just before the fire. Floyd claims he was at the boarding house talking to Freddy Ware, but Freddy says he came by as the fire siren was going off."

"Weell..." said Carrie.

"What is it, Maw?"

"Well, Floyd acted a little strange when he came over to the church steps. He asked Lily to forgive him, and I couldn't make sense of that. Then when we were in Lily's room I noticed the smell of smoke on him. But Jessie, I just can't believe Floyd would do such a thing. What reason would he have? That's how he makes his living, and I've always felt the orphanage is special to him. Nathan and Lissa think highly of him."

"What about Mary Carlisle?" asked Luke. "She's a strange one, but I can't see her doing something like that."

"Mary says she was at the boarding house with a headache, but there's no one to back up her story. Then Sarah McLindy told me she's seen Mary slipping out the side door of the boarding house several times at strange hours. The side door is right beside Mary's room, so she could easily slip out without being noticed. One of the times she saw her slipping out was the day the church fire was set."

"But what reason would she have?" asked Carrie.

"I don't know, Maw. She's a strange woman, as Luke said, and she has something from the past eating at her. I don't know that it's either her or Floyd, but I need to check into it further. I'm going to check into their backgrounds to see if that leads me anywhere. Most of the people who weren't in church just say they were at home, and that's hard to prove one way or the other. I don't want to think it's Floyd or Mary, but something about it keeps sticking in my craw. Needless to say, I don't want you to tell anyone what we've talked about, not even Nate or Syrena."

Jessie offered to take his mother home, but she wanted to walk. The day was warm for late September, and she needed to think. She found it impossible to believe Floyd or Mary could be the one setting the fires. Each had become like one of their family. Yet, she kept hearing Floyd on the day of the fire: "Please forgive me, Lily." Forgive him for what? How was she going to keep this from Nate? They never kept things from each other, but she had promised Jessie, and she would have to keep her word. Nate would understand.

Luke found some well-known carpenters, and they began work immediately on the orphanage. He still had the original plans for Alice's Hope, and they would follow those plans. Nathan would oversee the construction. He and Lissa had been keeping three of the orphans, and it had worked out so well they had decided to adopt them. The oldest was six and the youngest just eighteen months, so Lissa would have her hands full. A watchman was hired just to watch the orphanage, to make sure no fires were started while it was under construction.

It was a late afternoon in the middle of October when the fire siren began to scream once more. Everyone held their breath. Was it the orphanage? It was well underway now. Surely no one would set fire to it a second time.

Carrie and Nate had come in from the front porch, as the evenings were cooling quickly. Carrie had some sewing to do, and Nate was going to fix a squeaky board in the screened-in back porch. They both stopped their work, dread and fear taking over. What could it be? Could they get it out in time? Carrie began to pray.

It was thirty minutes before the telephone rang and Carrie heard Luke's voice.

"Maw, it's the boarding house!"

"Oh, no!" cried Carrie. "Why would anyone want to burn down the boarding house? Is Sarah all right?"

"Yes, she's fine. Maw, I want to come and get you and Papa Nate."

"Okay. But why, Luke? What are you not telling me?"

"I'll be there in just a few minutes," he answered.

They were at the bottom of the hill waiting when he arrived.

"Luke, is everyone all right?" asked Carrie, panic obvious in her voice.

"In a manner of speaking," replied Luke. "Can we just wait until we get there? I think you will understand better. The fire is out, Maw. It didn't do much damage. The watch team caught it in time. In fact, they saw her setting the fire."

They rode in silence for a few minutes, and then the word jumped out at Carrie. *Her.* Luke said they saw *her* setting the fire!

It seemed the entire town was outside the boarding house when Luke pulled in across the street and parked. The three of them got out of the car and walked toward the crowd. Something about the whole scene was strange, but Carrie's mind couldn't seem to comprehend what was going on. Luke said the fire was out, so why was everyone standing around looking at the boarding house? Then she realized everyone was looking up! As Carrie followed the direction of their eyes, her heart almost stopped. Someone was standing in a window on the top floor, precariously swaying from side to side! She felt Nate catch hold of her arm, as if to give her support. Who on earth was standing in the window? She shaded her eyes to see, and then her heart gave a lurch.

"Oh dear God...no!" she cried. "Mary! No!"

As she calmed enough to survey the scene, Carrie realized that someone was trying to talk to Mary.

"Mary, please come down. I don't want you to fall and hurt yourself. You are special to me, Mary. Please come down!"

It was Belinda.

Just then Jessie came to where Carrie, Nate and Luke were standing and watching.

"I've tried to talk to her, Maw. Then Belinda wanted to try. She won't talk to either of us. She just stands in the window like she's waiting for the courage to jump."

Carrie looked again at the pitiful figure poised on the window ledge.

"Let me try, Jessie."

"Okay, Maw. If anyone can get to her, it would be you. Just try not to upset her, or frighten her anymore than she already is."

Carrie walked past the crowd until she was under the window. Her throat was so tight the words would not come.

God, give me strength and the words.

"Mary!" she called. "Mary, it's Carrie. Would you come down so we can talk?"

There was no reply.

"Mary, it scares me to see you up there. I don't want anything to happen to you."

"You should have thought of that before you married Tom Swank."

Finally, a reply. But what did Mary mean by that?

"Mary, I'm not married to him now. He was not a good man, and I'm sorry about that. Did he hurt you in some way, Mary?"

"You don't even know who I am, do you?"

With this, Mary began to laugh: a terrible, disturbing laugh.

Carrie tried again.

"Mary, if you will come down, we will talk this over and you can explain it all to me. Then I will do my best to make up for whatever hurt Tom has caused you!"

Again, the laughing.

"You think you can just wave your magic wand and make everything all right! My whole life has been ruined, and you think you can just talk it into being right."

"I'll do everything in my power, Mary. Please come down. We care about you."

"You care about me! Nobody has cared about me since Papa died, and that was Tom Swank's fault. And if it was *his* fault, it was *your* fault, and *all* his family's fault. You had to pay. I had to take away things that meant something to you."

"Okay, Mary. I understand that you are hurt and angry. Please come down and tell me all about it. Tell me how Tom hurt you!"

"You don't even know who I am, do you?" she said for the second time.

With this, the horrible, demented laughing began again.

"I thought you told us you are Mary Carlisle! Is that not your name?"

"It's my name now, but I used to have a good, happy name. Don't you remember Mary Belle?"

Carrie gasped. She looked at Nate, then Luke, then Belinda.

Mary began to laugh harder.

"Now you're beginning to get it. Bet you haven't given Mary Belle a thought in years, have you? No one ever loved me but Papa Charles, and because of Tom Swank and my stupid mother, he died and left me. That's ALL YOUR FAULT!"

"Mary, come down and explain to me how it's my fault. I will listen and try to make amends."

"YOU CAN'T MAKE AMENDS!" Mary screamed, slinging her arms. She didn't sound like Mary anymore: she sounded like a madwoman.

"What can I do, Mary? Just tell me."

"You can't do anything except watch me die!" she screamed. "You can watch me die, and then you can remember that it's ALL YOUR FAULT! You can remember it the rest of your life."

As she talked, she kept turning lose of the window and waving her arms in anger. This sent chills through Carrie.

"Mary, if you will come down I will spend the rest of my life trying to help you. Belinda needs you to help her in the dress shop."

"Dress shop! Huh! That would have burned next! I just regret it's still standing."

"Okay, then we'll find something that makes you happy. Just come down."

"Why would I come down? To go to prison for the rest of my life? Or to an insane asylum? I've been in both, and I won't go back! Do you hear me? I WON'T GO BACK! There is no place for...oh...ohh..."

Mary, in her anger, lost her footing and came hurtling from the window to the rocky ground below. The volume of gasps from the crowd sounded like a roar, and parents covered their children's faces to shield them from the hideous sight.

Jessie and Luke rushed to where she lay; Carrie, Nate, and Belinda followed. Jessie knelt down and checked her, then looked up and shook his head. Mary was dead. Her pitiful, mangled body tore at Carrie's heart. This was Mary Belle, Paw Charles' little Mary Belle, who he had loved with his entire being. How could the sweet little girl they had once known turn into this?

Sarah McLindy came to Carrie, tears flowing.

"Oh, Carrie," she said, "I would never have thought this of Mary. Even after I told Jessie about her slipping out the side door, I felt there was a plausible reason. Come on in to the parlor and sit down. You look as if you're about to faint."

She and Nate led Carrie inside. As she sat on the sofa, Belinda, Ady Rose and Cindy also came inside. They all looked broken and scared. Lissa joined them.

"Aunt Carrie," she said, kneeling down beside the sofa. "I am so sorry. When I hired Mary, I never dreamed of anything like this. How could she blame you and your family for the way her life turned out?"

"She wasn't sane, Lissa," returned Carrie. "Somehow all the things that happened just messed up her mind. She had no..."

Suddenly she stopped, a thought suddenly hitting her.

"She was Nate's half-sister! Oh Nate, I never even thought of that! That must be why she looked at you so strangely the first time she met you."

Nate nodded. "I suppose you are right. Looks like I should have felt a connection somehow, but I didn't. I remember how much Paw Charles loved her. His face would light up when she came into the room."

Sarah brought tea into the parlor for all of them. They talked on for a bit as Carrie rested. It was getting dark and they all had families, so one by one they took their leave. Carrie was feeling calmer, so when Luke got to the boarding house, he suggested he take them home.

They insisted on walking by themselves from the bottom of the hill to the house.

"You need to get back to your family, Luke. They will have questions," said Nate. "I'll take good care of your mother."

Luke nodded, looking into Nate's eyes. "You always have, Papa Nate."

The next day Carrie and Nate stayed home, as they were both exhausted. The children called throughout the day to check on her. About mid-afternoon, Homer came by.

"I just wanted to check on you, Aunt Carrie," he said. "Are you okay?"

"Yes, dear," she replied. "I'm all right, just sad. It seems that Tom's misdoings will have no end. How long will people continue to suffer because of him? I'm glad, Dear, that Lily was not alive to have to witness this."

Homer smiled a sad smile. "Those were my first thoughts, when I saw Mary on that ledge. Lily really took up with her."

Jessie came by the next day. Carrie and Nate were braving the coolness of the October afternoon to just sit on the porch awhile. Her eyes brightened as her son came up the hill. *Tom did some bad things in his short life,* Carrie thought, *but he gave me six blessings. No one could have better children.*

Jessie sat down on the edge of the porch, his back against the banister. He looked absolutely worn out.

"Son, have you had any sleep?" asked Nate.

"Oh, some," Jessie answered. "I had to get everything checked out and get all the paperwork finished. Well, partly finished; I left Beady finishing up."

"Did you know it was her, Jessie?" asked Carrie.

"Not really. Not until yesterday. I had strongly suspected for a few days, but it was not until yesterday I felt sure. We were watching her, just waiting for her to set another fire. You see, she couldn't help but set more fires. She was so angry at everyone, and in her madness the fires were her way of releasing all that rage inside her."

Carrie let out a sigh. "She had such a terrible home life after Paw Charles died, a weak mother and an abusive stepfather. He's in prison now, thank God."

Jessie looked questioningly at his mother.

"In prison? Maw, her stepfather is not in prison. He's dead. He was murdered."

Carrie looked at her son blankly. Then she told him the story Mary had told her and the girls at the dress shop.

"Maw," said Jessie, after letting Carrie's story assimilate in his mind. "Only about half of that is true. Her stepfather did kill her mother after years of abuse, and he did run away from the scene and pass out in the woods. But he never woke up again, because someone stabbed him about six times in the chest."

Carrie sucked in her breath.

"Was it...?"

"They could never prove it," Jessie answered, shaking his head. "The next morning she showed up at the neighbors, not a speck of blood on her, but the sheriff over there always felt sure it was her. She was only eight years old. The sheriff said she never showed one ounce of emotion over her mother or her stepfather."

"What about her husband?" asked Carrie. "Did he die?"

"Yes, but again, under questionable circumstances. The police over in Kentucky thought she poisoned him, but they couldn't prove it."

"Oh my," said Carrie, shaking her head in disbelief. "Oh, my. Her whole life went awry because of Tom's sin. I can almost understand her hate, Jessie, and how it festered."

As Jessie sat there talking with them, they saw Homer coming up the hill. When he reached the porch, he greeted them and pulled up a chair.

"Aunt Carrie, we need to plan for Mary's funeral," he said. "After all, she is family, and no matter what she's done, she is one of God's children."

"You are right, Homer. Can we have her funeral in the church? I don't know if she had any money, but if not, Nate and I will pay for everything. Right, Nate?"

157

"As it turns out," said Homer, "she did have money. They found it in her room, almost five thousand dollars. She must have taken it from her husband when he died, before the police got to him. There will be plenty to cover the funeral. What about burial?"

This time Nate spoke. "We will bury her in Paw Charles' cemetery. She was his daughter, and it's exactly what he would have wanted."

Two days later, Mary Belle was laid to rest in the little Swank family cemetery beside her dear Papa Charles. Maw Izzy's grave was on the other side.

"I pray now she is at peace," said Carrie, "and that God will have mercy on her poor, confused, tormented soul."

CHAPTER 20

An overwhelming sadness settled in Carrie's heart over the next few days. She could see the sadness in Nate also, but neither talked about it. She knew they would later, but now there were no words for what had taken place.

On Sunday, Homer talked about love and forgiveness. He talked about the horrible life Mary had lived, and what that life had done to her.

"That is why it is so important to have God in your life," he said. "Mary did not have Him to help her through her trials. We tried to show her that love—and maybe we did to some extent—but her mind was already demented. We can be thankful we had the opportunity to show her our love, though, even if just for a little while. We cannot understand such things as this. We can only trust our Maker, and show more love for our fellow man."

After church, Sarah McLindy took Carrie by the arm and pulled her aside.

"Carrie, I need you to come by the boarding house this week, as soon as possible. I have something to show you, but please don't tell anyone!"

Carrie promised to go see her the next day, and she agreed to keep the meeting a secret. On the way home, she kept wondering what was so important. Sarah was not a busybody, and it wasn't like her to act in such a way, so Carrie knew it must be of consequence. She told Nate she wanted to go into town the next day, to visit Sarah and make sure she was all right after what had happened in her very own boarding house.

She arrived at Sarah's about ten o'clock, giving Sarah time to feed her boarders. Carrie had just reached out to knock when the door opened. Sarah stood there, wiping her hands on her apron.

"Come in, Carrie. Come in. I'm so glad you could come today. My heart has just been in a dither, wanting to show you what I have found. Come into my little sitting room. We can have some privacy there."

Carrie took a seat on the sofa as Sarah left the room for a moment. She reentered and handed Carrie a worn and dirty little brown book.

Confused, Carrie looked at the book and then at Sarah.

"Carrie," said Sarah, wringing her hands, "I've never done anything like this before, but I just did what I felt led to do. After Jessie came and looked through Mary's room and belongings, I went into her room to clean it up and change the linens and such. They were through with it, according to Jessie, so I will soon rent it out again. As I was changing the linens, I found this between the mattress and springs. It was pushed way back, so if Jessie did check, he could have missed it. Then, Carrie, I did something far out of my nature. I read it! Oh, I don't know what the Reverend would say about that!"

"What is it, Sarah?" asked Carrie, looking at the book, but afraid to open it.

"Well, I guess you would call it a diary," said Sarah, "though it's unlike any diary you have ever read. Just open it and read, Carrie."

Carrie reluctantly opened the diary. The first page was worn and dirty, the handwriting like that of a small child. She read the few words.

I don't like that man. He's dirty and smelly. Why does Mama let him come here?

Carrie looked up at Sarah, questioningly. That was all that was on the first page.

When Sarah said nothing, she turned to the next page. It was also smudged and dirty with childlike handwriting.

He came again tonight. He smelled like whiskey. I don't like him, and I don't like the way he looks at me.

The next page...

160

I am sad and I am angry. Mama says that old man is coming to live with us. Papa would be so mad at her. She's not my mama anymore.

The entries were not dated, but they must have been written when Mary was seven or eight years old. They were written with a dull pencil and dirty hands.

"See what I mean?" asked Sarah.

Carrie nodded and returned to the little book.

I won't call him 'Papa,' and he can't make me. He hit Mama real hard tonight. He hits her a lot, but tonight he knocked her down and I had to help her up. He laughed. I'll get even with him. I wish he was dead.

Carrie looked at Sarah, her eyes begging for some explanation. Sarah shook her head sadly.

"I chose not to show it to Jessie," said Sarah. "I want you to read it, Carrie. Then we will do with it whatever you say. I want you to take it home with you and read all of it. We will both pray about what we should do."

Carrie said goodbye to Sarah and left. Her mind felt absent from her body as she walked home. She would not tell Nate about the book—at least not until she read it all. When she arrived home, she went straight to her bedroom and sat down on the bed. Nate was helping Willy today, so she would have the privacy she needed. She looked at the book again, willing herself to read what was written there. Finally, she opened it and turned to the last page she had read. Then she turned to the next page.

I hate that old man more every day. I think I hate Mama, too, for letting him come here. She says they are married. Papa wouldn't like that at all. Yesterday he tied her to a stall in the barn and made her stay there all day just because he couldn't find his whiskey. He kept saying she did something with it. He dared me to even go near her, but while he went over the hill to get more whiskey, I took her some water and a biscuit.

Carrie continued to read. Each page showed Mary's mind creeping deeper and deeper into insanity. At places the pencil had been pressed so hard into the paper that it almost made a hole. She could see where wet spots had dried on the pages, and she knew they were Mary's tears. As she read, her tears mixed with Mary's.

I think all the time about him being dead. I would laugh to see him burning in hell. I can hear him yelling as he burns, and I almost laugh. I think about hitting him...and hitting him...and hitting him. It makes me feel good.

161

Carrie finally reached the last few pages.

I can't live with Mama and that old man anymore. I'm going to run away. If he kills Mama, I don't care anymore. She deserves it.

The next page...

Now it's really bad. Tonight he was drunk and mean. He twisted Mama's neck and threw her down on the floor, and she won't get up. I don't feel her breathing. I think she's dead. I don't really care. It's what she gets for marrying that old devil. He left, but I know where he is. He's got a place in the woods. I'm going after him.

The next page...

Well, he won't hurt nobody no more. It felt good to make him pay.

Carrie thought she had finished the book, but something else was written on the inside cover in the back...

I liked making him pay. Now some others have to pay.

Carrie closed the book, totally exhausted from the gravity of the words. How could a little girl feel such hatred? Her heart mourned for Mary's joyless childhood, and for the waste of so much talent. She could hear Mary's beautiful soprano voice. She held the book, wondering what to do.

Dear God, her heart cried, *when will this be over? When will Tom's sins stop tormenting us?*

Then a voice suddenly answered. *Now. It will end now.*

She sat there for a few minutes more, thinking, pondering, making sure. Then she arose from the bed without any further hesitation and headed toward the kitchen. At the old wood cook stove, she lifted the lid back and stirred the fire until the coals were red and bright. She looked at the book once more, then, without another thought, tossed it onto the coals. The flames shot up at the touch of the old dried-out pages. Carrie watched as the flames devoured the words, and she saw Mary's life before her. The flames ate up the sadness. They ate up the pain, the anger, the hatred, the desperation, the deranged thoughts. It was all gone in the flames, and as the flames finished their work, Carrie replaced the heavy stove lid and walked away, burdens lifted from her heart the way smoke had lifted from the flames.

The past was over. It was time to live, unhampered by what once was.

"We can't go forward and look back," she said aloud. "There is a season for everything, and this is the season for peace."

EPILOGUE

"What a beautiful fall day you have given us, Lord."

Carrie sat rocking on her front porch, enjoying a warm day in mid-October.

"Why, it must be seventy-five degrees."

There was a thermometer on the post of the porch, but Carrie's failing eyes couldn't make out its reading. She was talking aloud with no one there, but she didn't care.

"Why, if I live 'til my next birthday, I'll be ninety years old," she said out loud again. "I guess I've got a right to act a little senile. Not that I *want* to live 'til my next birthday, Lord. This living a long life is not what it's cracked up to be. I've seen too many go on to their reward while I'm still here hammering away at this life. Why, Lord, there's not anybody still here that's as old as I am. Don't you think it's time you called me on?"

My, my, she thought with wonder, *I've lived longer than anyone in my whole family.*

She smiled as she watched the new neighbors down below her, playing some sort of game in their yard. *Badminton, I think they call it,* she thought.

"New neighbors, my foot, Lord," she said aloud again. "They've been there nigh on ten years now."

They lived in the house where her good neighbors Harold and Nancy Moser used to live. Poor old Harold had passed from a heart attack, and he'd died right there in the yard where they were playing. It was no surprise when Nancy followed him three months later.

Carrie rocked some more as a tear slid down her cheek. She reached over and placed her hand on the rocking chair next to her. She could almost feel Nate's hand holding hers.

Nate's been gone almost ten years now, too. But look at me. I'm still here. It don't make any sense, Lord. I'm just telling you plain out, it don't make sense. I miss that man every minute of every day.

"No, it just don't make sense to me, Lord", she said aloud as she thumped the arm of her chair with her fist. "Now I'm not ungrateful, Lord. You let me have him for a long time. You gave me the best you had, and I thank you for that. I just wish you'd take me on, too, Lord, since I don't think you'll be bringing him back."

Most of Carrie's loved ones were gone: Lily, Nora, Ellie, all of her brothers. She was the last one living in her family. Even her other neighbors Henry and Lizzie Hankins were gone. Floyd was still living. They had given him a room at the orphanage to live out his years. He was blind as a bat now, but he constantly regaled the children with his funny stories.

"Grandma Carrie, don't you catch a chill."

Lainie, her great-granddaughter, placed a shawl around her shoulders and planted a kiss on her wrinkled old cheek. Carrie patted her hand to show her appreciation.

Lainie was Clay's granddaughter, from over in Kentucky. She had shown up on Carrie's doorstep one day, pregnant and no husband.

Pregnant, thought Carrie. *We never used that term back in my day. We said 'with child,' or 'in the family way.'*

Anyway, Lainie had left her home in Kentucky so as not to bring shame on her family. She had come to Carrie because she had been told all her life about what a good woman Carrie was, and how she showed love to everyone—and that's exactly what she found. Carrie took her in without one word of condemnation, and showed her love and understanding. The baby had been born prematurely, and had never drawn a breath in this world. The little girl was buried out in the new family cemetery, where Nate was buried. Once she was laid to rest, Lainie had just stayed on. Carrie was her family and this was her home, and Carrie had someone to take care of her.

You sure do know how to work things out, Lord, Carrie mused silently. *I guess I'll just keep trusting in your plan, even if I don't always understand it.*

Lainie went back inside and Carrie continued to rock and reminisce. All her children were well. That was definitely something to be thankful for.

"Papa Silas," she said, "I reckon I've even outdone you on the grand-children and great-grandchildren. I've got more than you can shake a stick at. If I remember right, after Luke and Syrena had little Caroline, I have sixteen grandchildren! Hoo-eee! That's a passel, ain't it, Papa!"

She laughed at Papa Silas' old saying. "Why, Papa, I've even got some great-great-grandchildren. Now, how about that? Don't ask me how many, though!"

She thought about all of her family and the lives they had made for themselves. Cindy's two boys had gone away and then returned. David had become a doctor and returned to his hometown about the time Doc White retired, and his twin brother Daniel had become Haymaker's first home-bred mortician.

I like that word, "mortician." It sounds better than "undertaker." Let's see... Carrie reminisced, *we've got teachers, farmers, nurses, businessmen and women, soldiers, ministers, horse trainers...and I don't even know what else. Yes, Lord, you have surely been good to us.*

Then there was Samuel: precious, precious Samuel. Carrie's heart leaped in her chest at the thought of him. Samuel had overcome the polio to some extent. *He was always a fighter,* she thought, laughing as she remembered. Samuel had always had to wear leg braces and use crutches as a result of the polio. Mr. Grayson had given him a job in his law office, and Samuel loved it. He had learned enough about the law to give even Mr. Grayson a run for his money, but he never got to be a lawyer. Carrie laid her head back and let her thoughts go back in time. *Dear Samuel. He lived to be twenty-three, and brought joy to everyone who knew him. But the pneumonia came, and his body was just too frail to fight it off. He was buried out there next to Nate, where I could keep an eye on them both; and I did.*

Carrie continued to rock. Her eyes turned to the cemetery where Nate was buried. She used to go out there at least twice a week and sit and talk to Nate, but her old legs just didn't want to hold up for the walk anymore. She missed talking to her darling Nate. He was such a good man; he'd just died in his sleep one night. Carrie had awakened to find him lifeless beside her. She never told anyone that she lay there and held him for an hour or more before she called for help.

"Yes, Lord, you gave me the very best," she said. "Now I'm ready anytime you are." Carrie continued to rock, waiting and singing.

"Amazing Grace, how sweet the sound, that saved a wretch like me...I once was lost but now I'm found, was blind but now I see..."

"I reckon you've been mighty good to me, Lord," she said, when she stopped singing. "Your grace is amazing, and it's been a good life. I know you'll come get me when you're ready."

Then she remembered one of her favorite scriptures from Ecclesiastes: *To everything there is a season, and time to every purpose under the heaven; A time to be born, and a time to die...*

Soon, Lord. Soon.

Carrie reached over to the rocker to take Nate's hand—and she smiled.

A MOUNTAIN WOMAN'S FAREWELL

The years have come and gone, Lord,
Filled with joy and her share of tears.
You've taught her to forgive, Lord,
And banished all her fears.

You gave her a home and family, Lord,
The desire of a woman's soul.
They filled her home with laughter,
Gave her warmth as she grew old.
Your mercy and grace abound, Lord;
Your perfect plan shines through.
Every day brings blessings and hope,
And a chance to begin anew.

But her heart is no longer in this world, Lord.
Her life's spanned nine years and fourscore.
Her longing is now for a new home, Lord.
She doesn't belong here anymore.
Now her thoughts turn upward;
Her eyes to the graveyard gate.
She hears him say, "I love you, my Carrie."
Oh, and I love you, my Nate.

— Brenda Crissman Musick

ABOUT THE AUTHOR

Brenda Crissman Musick was born in Southwest Virginia, in the small town of Honaker, and has happily spent her entire life there enjoying the beauty of the country and the friendliness of the people. There's no place on earth she would rather be. Her house has a big front porch where she and her husband wave at neighbors as they go by and watch the cows and calves across the way, often catching glimpses of foxes, deer, squirrels, wild turkeys, coyotes, and even a bear or two. She spent nineteen years teaching public school, taking early retirement to care for her father. She enjoyed teaching literature and getting students excited about poetry. Teaching was her passion and she loved every minute of it. She has also taught memoir and creative writing classes, symposium workshops, and she relishes speaking to groups about writing. Today she teaches adult Bible Studies, enjoys church work, writes, reads, and enjoys the little farm on which she and husband Jimmie live.

In addition to three novels, Brenda has written an illustrated children's book, *The Dolls on the Old Stairway*. She is a member of the Reminiscent Writers of SWCC and the Appalachian Authors Guild. She and Jimmie have three children: Chris, Cindy and Jacob, two daughters-in-law, one son-in-law, seven grandchildren, and recently added one grandson-in-law!

Contact Brenda at: musickb@jetbroadband.com, facebook.com/Brenda Crissman Musick, or by mail at P.O. Box 344, Honaker, VA 24260.